# DIFFICULTIES
## AND ALLEGED ERRORS
## AND CONTRADICTIONS
# IN THE BIBLE

By

R. A. Torrey

AUTHOR OF

*"What the Bible Teaches,"*
*"How to Work for Christ,"*
*"How to Pray,"* etc.

■

THE MOODY PRESS

153 Institute Place

CHICAGO

# INTRODUCTION

THIS book does not attempt to take up in detail every conceivable difficulty that could be found in the Bible. It would take many volumes to do that. I have simply taken up those objections of which the modern infidel makes the most, and which are most puzzling to many Christians. In going around the world, I have given people an opportunity to ask questions concerning matters that puzzle them. Pretty much everywhere I go, the questions are largely the same; and in this book I have taken up the questions which have been most frequently put to me, or which present apparently the greatest difficulties.

In regard to the questions which I have not touched upon, one can easily see that if so many difficulties are answered which they had supposed were unanswerable, the overwhelming probability is that all the other difficulties could be answered also if there were time and space to take them up.

*R. A. Torrey*

# CONTENTS

**1**

## A General Statement of the Case

Every careful student and every thoughtful reader of the Bible finds that the words of the apostle Peter concerning the Scriptures, that there are some things in them hard to be understood, which they that are unlearned and unstable wrest unto their own destruction (2 Peter 3:16), are abundantly true. Who is there of us who has not found things in the Bible that have puzzled us, yes, that in our early Christian experience have led us to question whether the Bible was, after all, the Word of God? We find some things in the Bible which it seems impossible for us to reconcile with other things in the Bible. We find some things which seem incompatible with the thought that the whole Bible is of divine origin and absolutely inerrant.

It is not wise to attempt to conceal the fact that these difficulties exist. It is the part of wisdom, as well as of honesty, to frankly face them and consider them.

What shall we say concerning these difficulties that every thoughtful student will sooner or later encounter?

1. *The first thing we have to say about these difficulties in the Bible is that from the very nature of the case difficulties are to be expected.*

Some people are surprised and staggered because there are difficulties in the Bible. For my part, I would be more surprised and staggered if there were not. What is the Bible? It is a revelation of the mind and will and character and being of an infinitely great, perfectly wise and absolutely holy God. God Himself is the Author of this revelation. But to whom is the revelation made? To men, to finite beings, to men who are imperfect in intellectual development and consequently in knowledge, and who are also imperfect in character and conse-

9

quently in spiritual discernment. The wisest man measured
on the scale of eternity is only a babe, and the holiest man
compared with God is only an infant in moral development.
There must, then, from the very necessities of the case, be
difficulties in such a revelation from such a source made to
such persons. When the finite tries to understand the infinite,
there is bound to be difficulty. When the ignorant contemplate
the utterances of one perfect in knowledge, there must be
many things hard to be understood, and some things which
to their immature and inaccurate minds appear absurd.
When beings whose moral judgments as to the hatefulness of
sin and as to the awfulness of the penalty that it demands
are blunted by their own sinfulness listen to the demands of
an absolutely holy Being, they are bound to be staggered at
some of His demands, and when they consider His dealings,
they are bound to be staggered at some of His dealings.
These dealings will appear too severe, too stern, too harsh,
too terrific.

It is plain that

### There Must be Difficulties

for as in such a revelation as the Bible has proven to be.[1]
If someone should hand me a book that was as simple to me
as the multiplication table, and say: "This is the Word of
God; in it He has revealed His whole will and wisdom," I
should shake my head and say: "I cannot believe it; that is
too easy to be a perfect revelation of infinite wisdom." There
must be in any complete revelation of God's mind and will
and character and being things hard for the beginner to
understand, and the wisest and best of us are but beginners.

2. *The second thing to be said about these difficulties is
that a difficulty in a doctrine, or a grave objection to a doctrine, does not in any wise prove the doctrine to be untrue.*

---

[1]Proof that the Bible is the Word of God may be found in the
author's book, *The Bible and Its Christ*

Many thoughtless people fancy that it does. If they come across some difficulty in the way of believing in the divine origin and absolute inerrancy and infallibility of the Bible, they at once conclude that the doctrine is exploded. That is very illogical. Stop a moment and think, and learn to be reasonable and fair. There is

SCARCELY A DOCTRINE IN SCIENCE GENERALLY BELIEVED TODAY

that has not had some great difficulty in the way of its acceptance.

When the Copernican theory, now so universally accepted, was first proclaimed, it encountered a very grave difficulty. If this theory were true, the planet Venus should have phases as the moon has, but no phases could be discovered by the best glass then in existence. But the positive argument for the theory was so strong that it was accepted in spite of this apparently unanswerable objection. When a more powerful glass was made, it was found that Venus had phases after all. The whole difficulty arose, as most all of those in the Bible arise, from man's ignorance of some of the facts in the case.

The nebular hypothesis is commonly accepted in the scientific world today. But when this theory was first announced, and for a long time afterward, the movements of the planet Uranus could not be reconciled with the theory. Uranus seemed to move in just the opposite direction from that in which it was thought it ought to move in accordance with the demands of the theory. But the positive arguments for the theory were so strong that it was accepted in spite of the inexplicable movements of Uranus.

If we apply to Bible study the common sense logic recognised in every department of science (with the exception of Biblical criticism, if that be a science), then we must demand that if the positive proof of a theory is conclusive, it must be believed by rational men in spite of any number of difficulties in minor details. He is a very shallow thinker indeed who gives up a well-attested truth because there are some apparent facts which he cannot reconcile with that truth. And he is a very shallow Bible scholar who gives up his belief in the divine origin and inerrancy of the Bible because there are some supposed facts that he cannot reconcile with that doctrine. There are in the theological world today many shallow thinkers of that kind.

3. *The third thing to be said about the difficulties in the Bible is that there are many more, and much greater, difficulties in the way of the doctrine that holds the Bible to be of human origin, and hence fallible, than there are in the way of the doctrine that holds the Bible to be of divine origin, and hence infallible.*

Oftentimes a man will bring you some difficulty and say: "How do you explain that, if the Bible is the Word of God?" and perhaps you may not be able to answer him satisfactorily. Then he thinks he has you cornered, but not at all. Turn on him, and ask him: "How do you account for the fulfilled prophecies of the Bible if it is of human origin? How do you account for the marvellous unity of the Book? How do you account for its inexhaustible depth? How do you account for its unique power in lifting men up to God? And so on." For every insignificant objection he can bring to your view of the Bible, you can bring very many more deeply significant objections to his view of the Bible. And any really candid man, who desires to know and obey the truth will have no difficulty in deciding between the two views.

Some time ago a young man, who was of a bright mind and unusually well read in sceptical and critical and agnostic literature, told me he had given the matter a great deal of candid and careful thought, and as a result he could not believe the Bible was of divine origin.

I asked him: "Why not?"

He pointed to a certain teaching of the Bible that he could not and would not believe to be true.

I replied: "Suppose for a moment that I could not answer that specific difficulty. that would not prove that the Bible is not of divine origin. I can bring you many things far more difficult to account for on the hypothesis that the Bible is not of divine origin than this is on the hypothesis that the Bible is of divine origin. You cannot deny the fact of fulfilled prophecy. How do you account for it if the Bible is not God's Word? You cannot shut your eyes to the marvellous unity of the sixty-six books of the Bible, written under such divergent circumstances and at periods of time so remote from one another. How do you account for it, if God is not the real Author of the Book back of the forty or more human authors? You cannot deny that the Bible has a power to save men from sin, to bring men peace and hope and joy, to lift men up to God, that all other books taken together do not possess. How do you account for it if the Bible is not the Word of God in a sense that no other book is the Word of God?"

The objector did not answer. The difficulties that confront one who denies that the Bible is of divine origin and authority are far more numerous and vastly more weighty than those which confront the one who believes it to be of divine origin and authority.

4. *The fourth thing to be said about the difficulties in the Bible is: the fact that you cannot solve a difficulty does not prove it cannot be solved, and the fact that you cannot answer an objection does not prove at all that it cannot be answered.*

It is remarkable how often we overlook this very evident fact. There are many, who, when they meet a difficulty in the Bible and give it a little thought and can see no possible solution, at once jump at the conclusion that a solution is impossible by anyone, and so they throw up their faith in the inerrancy of the Bible and in its divine origin. It would seem as if any man would have a sufficient amount of that modesty that is becoming in beings so limited in knowledge as we all undeniably are to say:

"Though I see no possible solution to this difficulty, some-one a little wiser than I might easily find one."

If we would only bear in mind that we do not know everything, and there are a great many things that we cannot solve now that we could very easily solve if we only knew a little more, it would save us from all this folly. Above all, we ought never to forget that there may be a very easy solution to infinite wisdom even to that which to our finite wisdom — or ignorance — appears absolutely insoluable. What would we think of a beginner in algebra, who, having tried in vain for half an hour to solve a difficult problem, declared that there was no possible solution to the problem because he could find none?

A man of unusual experience and ability one day left his work and came a long distance to see me in great perturbation of spirit because he had discovered what seemed to him a flat contradiction in the Bible. He had lain awake all night thinking about it. It had defied all his attempts at reconciliation, but when he had fully stated the case to me, in a very few moments I showed him a very simple and satisfactory solution of the difficulty. He went away with a happy heart. But why had it not occurred to him at the outset that though it appeared absolutely impossible to him to find a solution after all a solution might be easily discovered by someone else? He supposed that the difficulty was an entirely new one, but it was one that had been faced and answered long before either he or I was born.

5. *The fifth thing to be said about the difficulties in the Bible is that the seeming defects of the Book are exceedingly insignificant when put in comparison with its many and marvellous excellencies.*

It certainly reveals great perversity of both mind and heart that men spend so much time expatiating on such insignificant points that they consider defects in the Bible, and pass absolutely unnoticed the incomparable beauties and wonders that adorn and glorify almost every page. Even in some prominent institutions of learning, where men are supposed to be taught to appreciate and understand the Bible and where they are sent to be trained to preach its truth to others, much more time is spent on minute and insignificant points that seem to point toward an entirely human origin of the Bible than is spent upon studying and understanding and admiring the unparalleled glories that make this Book stand apart from all other books in the world. What would we think of any man who in studying some great master-piece of art concentrated his whole attention upon what looked like a fly-speck in the corner? A large proportion of the much vaunted "critical study of the Bible" is a laborious and scholarly investigation of supposed fly-specks. The man who is not willing to squander the major portion of his time in this erudite investigation of fly-specks but prefers to devote it to the study of the unrivalled beauties and ma-jestic splendors of the Book is counted in some quarters as not being "scholarly and up to date."

6. *The sixth thing to be said about the difficulties in the Bible is that they have far more weight with superficial read-ers than with profound students.*

Take a man like the late Colonel Ingersoll, who was totally ignorant of the real contents and meaning of the Bible, or that class of modern preachers who read the Bible for the most part for the sole purpose of finding texts to serve as pegs to hang their own ideas upon. To such super-ficial readers of the Bible these difficulties seem of immense importance, but to the one who has learned to meditate upon the Word of God day and night they have scarcely any weight at all. That rare man of God, George Müller, who had carefully studied the Bible from beginning to end more than one hundred times, was not disturbed by any difficul-ties he encountered, but to the man who is reading it through for the first or second time there are many things that per-plex and stagger.

7. *The seventh thing to be said about the difficulties in the Bible is that they rapidly disappear upon careful and prayer-ful study.*

How many things there are in the Bible that once puzzled and staggered us, but which have since been perfectly cleared up and no longer present any difficulty whatever! Every year of study finds these difficulties disappear more and more rapidly. At first they go by ones, and then by twos, and then by dozens, and then by scores. Is it not reasonable then to suppose that the difficulties that still remain will all disappear upon further study?

### CLASSES OF DIFFICULTIES

ALL the difficulties found in the Bible can be included under ten general heads.

1. *The first class of difficulties: those that arise from the text from which our English Bible was translated.*

No one, as far as I know, holds that the English translation of the Bible is absolutely infallible and inerrant. The doctrine held by many is that the Scriptures *as originally given* were absolutely infallible and inerrant, and that our English translation is a *substantially accurate* rendering of the Scriptures as originally given. We do not possess the original manuscripts of the Bible. These original manuscripts were copied many times with great care and exactness, but naturally some errors crept into the copies that were made. We now possess so many good copies that by comparing one with another, we can tell with great precision just what the original text was. Indeed, for all practical purposes the original text is now settled. There is not one important doctrine that hangs upon any doubtful reading of the text. But when our Authorised Version was made some of the best manuscripts were not within reach of the translators, and the science of textual criticism was not so well understood as it is today, and so the translation was made from an imperfect text. Not a few of the apparent difficulties in the Bible arise from this source.

For example, we are told in John 5:4 that "an angel went down at a certain season into the pool, and troubled the water: whosoever then first after the troubling of the water stepped in was made whole of whatsoever disease he had." This statement for many reasons seems improbable and difficult to believe, but upon investigation we find that it is all a mistake of the copyist. Some early copyist, reading John's account, added in the margin his explanation of the healing properties of this intermittent medicinal spring. A late copyist embodied this marginal note in the body of the text, and so it came to be handed down and got into the Authorized Version. Very properly it has been omitted from the Revised Version.

The discrepancies in figures in different accounts of the same events, as, for example, the differences in the ages of some of the kings as given in the text of Kings and Chronicles, doubtless arise from the same cause, errors of copyists. Such an error in the matter of figures would be very easy to make, as in the Hebrew numbers are denoted by letters, and letters that appear very much alike have a very different value as figures. For example, the first letter in the Hebrew alphabet denotes one, and with two little points above it, not larger than fly-specks, it denotes a thousand. The twenty-third or last letter of the Hebrew alphabet denotes four hundred, but the eighth letter of the Hebrew alphabet, that looks very much like it and could be easily mistaken for it, denotes eight. A very slight error of the copyist would therefore make an utter change in figures. The remarkable thing when one contemplates the facts in the case is that so few errors of this kind have been made.

2. *The second class of difficulties: those that arise from inaccurate translations.*

For example, in Matthew 12:40 Jonah is spoken of as being in "the whale's belly." Many a sceptic has made merry over the thought of a whale with the peculiar construction of its mouth and throat swallowing a man, but if the sceptic had only taken the trouble to look the matter up, he would have found the word translated "whale" really means "sea monster," without any definition as to the character of the sea monster. We will take this up more in detail in considering the story of Jonah. So the whole difficulty arose from the translator's mistake and the sceptic's ignorance. There are many sceptics today who are so densely ignorant of matters clearly understood by many Sunday school children that they are still harping in the name of scholarsnip on this supposed error in the Bible.

3. *The third class of difficulties: those that arise from false interpretations of the Bible.*

What the Bible teaches is one thing, and what men interpret it to mean is oftentimes something widely different. Many difficulties that we have with the Bible arise not from what the Bible actually says, but from what men interpret it to mean.

A striking illustration of this is found in the first chapter of Genesis. If we were to take the interpretation put upon this chapter by many interpreters, it would indeed be difficult to reconcile it with much that modern science regards as established. But the difficulty is not with what the first chapter of Genesis says, but with the interpretation that is put upon it. But there is no contradiction whatever between what is really proven by science and what is really said in the first chapter of Genesis. This will come out clearly in the chapter that follows on "The First Chapter of Genesis."

Another difficulty of the same character is with Jesus' statement that He would be three days and three nights in the heart of the earth. Many interpreters would have us believe that He died Friday night and rose early Sunday morning, and the time between these two is far from being three days and three nights; but we shall see later that it is a matter of Biblical interpretation, and the trouble is not with what the Bible actually says, but with the interpretation that men put upon the Bible. We will take this matter up at length in the chapter "Was Jesus Actually Three Days and Three Nights in the Heart of the Earth?"

4. *The fourth class of difficulties: those that arise from a wrong conception of the Bible.*

Many think that when you say the Bible is the Word of God, of divine origin and authority, you mean that God is the speaker in every utterance it contains; but this is not at all what is meant. Oftentimes it simply records what others say,—what good men say, what bad men say, what inspired men say, what uninspired men say, what angels and demons say, and even what the devil himself says. The record of what they said is from God and absolutely true, but what those other persons are recorded as saying may be true or may not be true. It is true that they said it, but what they said may not be true.

For example, the devil is recorded in Genesis 3:4 as saying: "Ye shall not surely die." It is true that the devil said it, but what the devil said is not true, but an infamous lie that shipwrecked our race. That the devil said it is God's Word, but what the devil said is not God's word but the devil's word. It is God's Word that this was the devil's word.

Very many careless readers of the Bible do not notice who is talking—God, good men, bad men, inspired men, uninspired men, angels or devil. They will tear a verse right out of its context regardless of the speaker and say: "There, God said that," but God said nothing of the kind. God's Word says that the devil said it, or a bad man said it, or a good man said it, or an inspired man said it, or an uninspired man said it, or an angel said it. What God says is true, namely, that the devil said it, or a bad man, or a good man, or an inspired man, or an uninspired man, or an angel. But what they said may or may not be true.

It is very common to hear men quote what Eliphaz, Bildad, or Zophar said to Job as if it were necessarily God's own words because it is recorded in the Bible, in spite of the fact that God disavowed their teaching and said to them: "Ye have not spoken of Me the thing which is right" (Job 42:7). It is true that these men said the thing that God records them as saying, but oftentimes they gave the truth a twist and said what is not right. A very large share of our difficulties thus arises from not noticing who is speaking. The Bible always tells us, and we should always note it.

In the Psalms we have sometimes what God said to man, and that is always true, but on the other hand, we often have what man said to God, and that may or may not be true. Sometimes, and far oftener than most of us see, it is the voice of the speaker's personal vengeance or despair. This vengeance may be and often is prophetic, but it may be the wronged man committing his cause to Him to whom vengeance belongeth (Romans 12:19), and we are not obliged to defend all that he said. In the Psalms we have even a record of what the fool said, namely: "There is no God" (Psalm 14:1). Now it is true that the fool said it, but the fool lied when he said it. It is God's Word that the fool said it, but what God reports the fool as saying is not God's own word at all but the fool's own word.

So in studying our Bible, if God is the speaker we must believe what He says. If an inspired man is the speaker we must believe what he says. If an uninspired man is the speaker we must judge for ourselves—it is perhaps true, perhaps false. If it is the devil who is speaking, we do well to remember that he was a liar from the beginning, but even the devil may tell the truth sometimes.

5. *The fifth class of difficulties: those that arise from the language in which the Bible was written.*

The Bible is a book for all ages and for all kinds of people, and therefore it was written in the language that continues the same and is understood by all, the language of the common people and of appearances. It was not written in the terminology of science.

Thus, for example, what occurred at the battle of Gibeon (Joshua 10:12-14) was described in the way it appeared to those who saw it, and the way in which it would be understood by those who read about it. There is no talk about the refraction of the sun's rays, and so forth, but the sun is said to have *"stood still"* (or tarried) in the midst of heaven. It is one of the perfections of the Bible that it was not written in the terminology of modern science. If it had been, it would never have been understood until the present day, and even now it would be understood only by a few. Furthermore, as science and its terminology are constantly changing, the Bible if written in the terminology of the science of to-day would be out of date in a few years, but being written in just the language chosen it has proved the Book for all ages, all lands and all conditions of men.

Other difficulties from the language in which the Bible was written arise from the fact that large portions of the Bible are poetical and are written in the language of poetry, the language of feeling, passion, imagination and figure. Now if a man is hopelessly prosaic, he will inevitably find difficulties with these poetical portions of the inspired Word.

For example, in Psalm 18 we have a marvellous description of a thunderstorm, but let the dull, prosaic fellow get hold of that, for example the 8th verse: "There went up a smoke out of His nostrils, and fire out of His mouth devoured: coals were kindled by it," and he will be head over heels in difficulty at once. But the trouble is not with the Bible, but with his own stupid, thick-headed prosaicness.

6. *The sixth class of difficulties: those that arise from our defective knowledge of the history, geography and usages of Bible times.*

For example, in Acts 13:7 Luke speaks of "the deputy" (or, more accurately, "the proconsul," see Revised Version) of Cyprus. Roman provinces were of two classes, imperial and senatorial. The ruler of the imperial provinces was called a "propraetor," of a senatorial province a "proconsul." Up to a comparatively recent date, according to the best information we had, Cyprus was an imperial province and therefore its ruler would be a "propraetor," but Luke calls him a "proconsul." This certainly seemed like a clear case of error on Luke's part, and even the conservative commentators felt forced to admit that Luke was in slight error, and the destructive critics were delighted to find this "mistake." But further and more thorough investigation has brought to light the fact that just at the time of which Luke wrote the senate had made an exchange with the emperor whereby Cyprus had become a senatorial province, and therefore its ruler a proconsul; and Luke was right after all, and the literary critics were themselves in error.

Time and time again further researches and discoveries, geographical, historical and archæological, have

## VINDICATED THE BIBLE

and put to shame its critics. For example, the book of Daniel has naturally been one of the books that infidels and destructive critics have most hated. One of their strongest arguments against its authenticity and veracity was that such a person as Belshazzar was unknown to history, and that all historians agreed that Nabonidus was the last king of Babylon, and that he was absent from the city when it was captured; and so Belshazzar must be a purely mythical character, and the whole story legendary and not historical. Their argument seemed very strong. In fact, it seemed unanswerable. But Sir H. Rawlinson discovered at Mugheir and other Chaldean sites clay cylinders on which Belshazzar (Belsaruzur) is named by Nabonidus as his eldest son. Doubtless he reigned as regent in the city during his father's absence, an indication of which we have in his proposal to make Daniel third ruler in the kingdom (Daniel 5:16)—he himself being second ruler in the kingdom, Daniel would be next to himself. So the Bible was vindicated and the critics put to shame.

It is not so long since the destructive critics asserted most positively that Moses could not have written the Pentateuch because writing was unknown in his day, but recent discoveries have proved beyond a question that writing far antedates the time of Moses. So the destructive critics have been compelled to give up their argument, though they have had the bad grace to hold on stubbornly to their conclusion.

7. *The seventh class of difficulties: those that arise from the ignorance of conditions under which books were written and commands given.*

For example, to one ignorant of the conditions God's commands to Israel as to the extermination of the Canaanites, seem cruel and horrible, but when one understands the moral condition to which these nations had sunken, and the utter hopelessness of reclaiming them, and the weakness of the Israelites themselves, their extermination seems to have been an act of mercy to all succeeding generations and to themselves. We will go into this more fully in the chapter on "The Slaughter of the Canaanites."

8. *The eighth class of difficulties: those that arise from the many-sidedness of the Bible.*

The broadest minded man is one-sided, but the truth is many-sided, and the Bible is all-sided. So to our narrow thought one part of the Bible seems to contradict another.

For example, men as a rule are either Calvinistic or Arminian in their mental make-up, and some portions of the Bible are decidedly Calvinistic and present great difficulties to the Arminian type of mind, while other portions are decidedly Arminian and present difficulties to the Calvinistic type of mind. But

BOTH SIDES ARE TRUE.

Many men in our day are broad-minded enough to be able to grasp at the same time the Calvinistic side of the truth and the Arminian side of the truth, but some are not, and so the Bible perplexes, puzzles and bewilders them,—but the trouble is not with the Bible, but with their own lack of capacity for comprehensive thought.

So, too, Paul seems to contradict James, and James seems sometimes to contradict Paul, and what Paul says in one place seems to contradict what he says in another place. But the whole trouble is that our narrow minds cannot take in God's large truth.

9. *The ninth class of difficulties: those that arise from the fact that the Bible has to do with the infinite, and our minds are finite.*

It is necessarily difficult to put the facts of infinite being into the limited capacity of our finite intelligence, just as it is difficult to put the ocean into a pint cup. To this class of difficulties belong those connected with the Bible doctrine of the Trinity and with the Bible doctrine of the divine-human nature of Christ. To those who forget that God is infinite, the doctrine of the Trinity seems like the mathematical monstrosity of making one equal three. But when one bears in mind that the doctrine of the Trinity is an attempt to put into forms of finite thought the facts of infinite being, and into material forms of expression the facts of the spirit, the difficulties vanish. The simplicity of the Unitarian conception of God arises from its shallowness.

10. *The tenth class of difficulties: those that arise from the dullness of our spiritual perceptions.*

The man who is farthest advanced spiritually is still so immature that he cannot expect to see everything yet as an absolutely holy God sees it, unless he takes it upon simple faith in Him. To this class of difficulties belong those connected with the Bible doctrine of eternal punishment. It oftentimes seems to us as if this doctrine cannot be true, must not be true, but the whole difficulty arises from the fact that we are still so blind spiritually that we have no adequate conception of the awfulness of sin, and especially of the awfulness of the sin of rejecting the infinitely glorious Son of God. But when we become so holy, so like God, that we see the enormity of sin as He sees it, we shall have no difficulty with the doctrine of eternal punishment.

As we look back over the ten classes of difficulties, we see

### They All Arise from Our Imperfection

and not from the imperfection of the Bible. The Bible is perfect, but we, being imperfect, have difficulty with it. As we grow more and more into the perfection of God, our difficulties grow ever less and less, and so we are forced to conclude that when we become as perfect as God is, we shall have no more difficulties whatever with the Bible.

## III

How Shall We Deal with the Difficulties of the Bible?

Before taking up those specific difficulties and alleged "contradictions" in the Bible which have caused the most trouble to seekers after truth, let us first consider how difficulties in general should be dealt with.

1. *First of all, let us deal with them honestly.*
Whenever you find a difficulty in the Bible frankly acknowledge it. Don't try to obscure it. Don't try to dodge it. Look it square in the face. Admit it frankly to whoever mentions it. If you cannot give a good, square, honest explanation, do not attempt any at all. Untold harm has been done by those who in their zeal for the infallibility of the Bible have attempted explanations of difficulties which do not commend themselves to the honest, fair-minded man. People have concluded that if these are the best explanations, then there are really no explanations at all, and the Bible instead of being helped has been injured by the unintelligent zeal of foolish friends. If you are not really convinced that the Bible is the Word of God, you can far better afford to wait for an honest solution of a difficulty than you can afford to attempt a solution that is evasive and unsatisfactory.

2. *In the second place, let us deal with them humbly.*
Recognize the limitations of your own mind and knowledge, and do not for a moment imagine that there is no solution just because you have found none. There is, in all probability, a very simple solution, even when you can find no solution at all.

3. *In the third place, deal with the difficulty determinedly.*
Make up your mind that you will find the solution if you can by any amount of study and hard thinking. The difficul-

ties of the Bible are our heavenly Father's challenge to us to set our brains to work. Do not give up searching for a solution because you cannot find one in five minutes or ten minutes. Ponder over it and work over it for days if necessary. The work will do you more good than the solution does. There is a solution somewhere, and you will find it if you will only search for it long enough and hard enough.

4. *In the fourth place, deal with the difficulty fearlessly.*

Do not be frightened when you find a difficulty, no matter how unanswerable or how insurmountable it appears at first sight. Thousands of men have found just such difficulties

### Before You Were Born.

They were seen hundreds of years ago, and still the old Book stands. The Bible that has stood eighteen centuries of rigid examination, and also of incessant and awful assault, is not likely to go down before your discoveries or before the discharges of any modern critical guns. To one who is at all familiar with the history of critical attacks on the Bible, the confidence of those modern destructive critics who think they are going to annihilate the Bible at last, is simply amusing.

5. *In the fifth place, deal with the difficulty patiently.*

Do not be discouraged because you do not solve every problem in a day. If some difficulty persistently defies your very best efforts at a solution, lay it aside for a while. Very likely when you come back to it, it will have disappeared and you will wonder how you were ever perplexed by it.

6. *In the sixth place, deal with the difficulty Scripturally.*

If you find a difficulty in one part of the Bible, look for other Scripture to throw light upon it and dissolve it. Nothing explains Scripture like Scripture. Time and again people have come to me with some difficulty in the Bible that had greatly staggered them, and asked for a solution, and I have been able to give a solution by simply asking them to read some other chapter and verse, and the simple reading of that chapter and verse has thrown such a light upon the passage in question that all the mists have disappeared and the truth has shone as clear as day.

7. *In the seventh place, deal with the difficulty prayerfully.* It is simply wonderful how difficulties dissolve when one looks at them on his knees. Not only does God open our eyes in answer to prayer to behold wonderful things out of His law, but He also opens our eyes to look straight through a difficulty that before we prayed seemed impenetrable. One great reason why many modern Bible scholars have learned to be destructive critics is because they have forgotten how to pray.

# IV

## Is the First Chapter of Genesis Historical and Scientific?

There is no part of the Bible that the more scholarly opponents of its divine origin are more fond of attacking than the very first chapter in the Book. Time and again have we been assured that the teachings of this chapter are in hopeless conflict with the best established conclusions of modern science. Even a prominent theological teacher in a supposedly Christian university has said that "no one who knows what history and science are would think of calling the first chapter of Genesis either historical or scientific." But in spite of this confident assertion, men who have gained a name as historians beyond anything that this teacher of theology can expect, assure us that it is not only historical but the very foundation of history. Other men, who have secured for themselves a position in the scientific world to which this teacher can never hope to aspire, assure us that this chapter agrees absolutely with everything that is known scientifically of the origin and early history of the earth. For example, there is no name more honored in the scientific world today than that of Lord Kelvin. Lord Kelvin, in a private letter to a friend of mine, says:

"Physical science has nothing to say against the order of creation as given in Genesis."

But let us come to the specific difficulties in the first chapter of Genesis.

The objector is fond of telling us that "the first chapter of Genesis says that the world was created in six days of twenty-four hours each, when everyone who is familiar with modern science knows that the world as it now stands was millions of years in the making."

This objection sounds well, but the one who makes it displays a hopeless ignorance of the Bible. Anyone who is at

29

all familiar with the Bible and the Bible usage of words knows that the word "day" is

## Not Limited to Periods of Twenty-four Hours.

It is frequently used of a period of time of an entirely undefined length. For example, in Joel 3:18-20 the millennial period is spoken of as a "day." In Zechariah 2:10-13 the millennial period is again spoken of as a "day," and again in Zechariah 13:1, 2 and 14:9. Even in the second chapter of Genesis the whole period covered by the six days of the first account is spoken of as a "day" (Genesis 2:4, 5). There is no necessity whatever for interpreting the days of Genesis 1 as solar days of twenty-four hours each. They may be vast periods of undefined length.

But someone may say: "This is twisting the Scriptures to make them fit the conclusions of modern science."

The one who says so simply displays his ignorance of the history of Biblical interpretation. St. Augustine, as far back as the fourth century, centuries before modern science and its conclusions were dreamed of, interpreted the days of Genesis 1 as periods of time, just what the word means in many places elsewhere in the Bible.

Another point urged against the truth and accuracy of the account of creation given in Genesis 1 is that it speaks of "there being light before the sun existed, and it is absurd to think of light before the sun, the source of light."

The one who says this displays his ignorance of modern science. Anyone who is familiar with the nebular hypothesis, commonly accepted among scientific men today, knows that there was cosmic light ages before the sun became differentiated from the general luminous nebulous mass as a separate body.

But the objector further urges against the scientific accuracy of Genesis 1 that its order of creation is not the order determined by the investigations of modern science.

This is an assertion that cannot be proven. It was the writer's privilege to study geology under that prince of geologists, who has been pronounced by competent authority to be the greatest scientific thinker of the nineteenth century with the exception of Charles Darwin, namely, Professor James D. Dana of Yale. Professor Dana once said in my presence that "one reason why he believed the Bible to be the Word of God was because of the marvellous accord of the order of creation given in Genesis with that worked out by the best scientific investigation." Note also what Lord Kelvin is quoted as saying in the early part of this chapter.

It must be said, however, that men of science are constantly changing their views of what was the exact order of creation. Very recently discoveries have been made that have overthrown theories of the order of creation held by many men of science and which did not seem to some to harmonize with the order as given in the first chapter of Genesis, but these recent discoveries have brought the order into harmony with the order as given in that chapter.

There is no need of going in detail into this order of creation as taught by modern science and taught in Genesis 1. For there is grave reason to doubt if anything in Genesis 1 after verse 1 relates to the original creation of the universe. All the verses after the first seem rather to refer to

## A REFITTING OF THE WORLD

that had been created and had afterwards been plunged into chaos by the sin of some pre-Adamic race, to be the abode of the present race that inhabits it, the Adamic race.

The reasons for so thinking are, first, that the words translated "without form and void" (R. V., "waste and void") are used everywhere else in the Bible of the state of affairs that God brought upon persons and places as a punishment for sin. For example, in Isaiah 34:11 we read of the judgment that God shall bring upon Idumea as a punishment for their sins in these words: "He shall stretch over it a line of confusion, and the plummet of emptiness" (R. V.). The Hebrew words translated "confusion" and "emptiness" are the same that are translated "without form and void" in Genesis 1:2.

We read again in Jeremiah 4:23-27: "I beheld the earth, and, lo, it was waste and void." In both instances the words "waste and void" refer to a ruin which God had sent as a punishment for sin, and the assumption is very strong that they have a similar significance in Genesis 1.

The second reason for this interpretation is stronger yet, namely, that the Bible expressly declares that God did not create the earth "in vain" (Isaiah 45:18). But the word translated "in vain" in this passage is precisely the one translated "without form" in Genesis 1:2. In the Revised Version of Genesis 1:2 and Isaiah 45:18 the word is translated in both instances "waste." Here then is a plain and specific declaration in the Bible that God did not create the earth "without form" (or rather "waste," R. V.), so it is plain that Genesis 1:2 cannot refer to the original creation. The word translated "was" in Genesis 1:2 can, with perfect propriety, be translated "became," then Genesis 1:2 would read: "And the earth became waste and void." In that case in Genesis 1:1 we have the actual account of creation. It is very brief but wonderfully expressive, instructive and suggestive. In Genesis 1:2 we have a brief but suggestive account of how the earth became involved in desolation and emptiness, presumably through the sin of some pre-Adamic race. Then all after verse 2 does not describe the original creation of the earth, but its fitting up anew for the new race God is to bring upon the earth—the Adamic race. Even if we allow the word "was" to stand in Genesis 1:2, and do not substitute the word "became," it does not materially affect the interpretation.

If this be the true interpretation of the chapter (and the argument for this interpretation seems conclusive), then of course this record cannot by any possibility come into conflict with any discoveries of geology as yet made or to be made, for the geological strata lie back of the period here described. The agreement of the order as set forth in Genesis 1 with the order as discovered by science would be accounted for by the fact that God always works in orderly progress from the lower to the higher.

## V

### THE ANTIQUITY OF MAN ACCORDING TO THE BIBLE AND ACCORDING TO SCIENCE

ONE of the questions that is greatly puzzling many Bible scholars today is how to reconcile the chronology of the Bible with discoveries that are being made as to the antiquity of man. It is said that the Bible chronology only allows about 4000 years from Adam to Christ, but the Egyptian and Babylonian civilizations were highly developed before 4000 years before Christ. If there were but 4000 years from Adam to Christ there would be only 5907 years for the whole age of the whole human race, and historians and scientists are thought to have traced the history of the race back 10,000 or more years. How are we to reconcile these apparent discrepancies?

In the first place, let it be said that *the dates commonly accepted by many historians are not at all certain.*

For example, in figuring out the dates of Egyptian dynasties the data upon which conclusions are built can hardly be considered decisive. It is true, discoveries have been made of ancient records which assert that the dynasties which preceded them covered certain vast periods of time which are named, but anyone who is at all familiar with the ancient and oriental habit of exaggeration should receive these assertions as to the length of these dynasties with a great deal of caution. While these views of the vast antiquity of the ancient Egyptian civilization and ancient civilizations of Nineveh and Babylon, as well, are widely accepted, they are not by any means proven. We can afford to wait for more light.

On the other hand, *it is not at all sure that there were only about 4000 years from Adam to Christ.*

Bishop Ussher's chronology, which is found in the margin of most reference Bibles, is not a part of the Bible itself, and its accuracy is altogether doubtful. It is founded upon the supposition that the genealogies of Scripture are intended to be complete, but a careful study of these genealogies clearly shows they are not intended to be complete, that they oftentimes contain only some outstanding names. For example, the genealogy in Exodus 6:16-24, if it were taken as a complete genealogy containing all the names, would make Moses the great-grandson of Levi, though 430 years intervened. Again there is reason to question whether the lists of names in Genesis 5 and 11 are complete. "The total length of time from Adam to the flood and from the flood to Abraham is never mentioned in Scripture, although the period from Joseph to Moses (Exodus 12:40) and that from the Exodus to the building of the temple (1 Kings 6:1) are mentioned." "The fact that there are just ten names in each list also suggests that a similar arrangement may have been made in the first chapter of Matthew." The regular formula is: "A lived —— years and begat B. And A lived after he begat B —— years and begat sons and daughters. B lived —— years and begat C," etc. The word translated "begat" is sometimes used not of an immediate descendant but of succeeding generations. For example, Zilpah is said to have borne her great-grandchildren (Genesis 46:18). The Hebrew word translated "bare" in this passage is the same word translated "begat" in the other passages. Bilhah is said to have borne her grandchildren (Genesis 46:25). Canaan is said to have begotten whole nations (Genesis 10:15-18). So we see that in the formula quoted above the meaning is not necessarily that B is the literal son of A. B may be his literal son or a distant descendant. Thus many centuries may have intervened between A and B. Of course, no chronology is intended by these figures. Their purpose is not at all to show the age of the world. We see, therefore, there is no real and necessary conflict betwen real Bible chronology and any modern historical discoveries as to the antiquity of man.

It should be said further that *it may be that these ancient civilizations which are being discovered in the vicinity of Nineveh and elsewhere may be the remains of the pre-Adamic race already mentioned.*

There are passages in the Bible which seem to hint that there were some existing even in Bible times who may have belonged to these pre-Adamic races. Such may have been the Rephaim and Zamzummin and the Emim (see Genesis 14:5, R. V.; Deuteronomy 2:20, 21; 3:11, A. V. and R. V.). The hints given in those passages are somewhat obscure, but seem to suggest the remains of a race other than the Adamic race. If such was the case, these earlier civilizations which are now being uncovered may have been theirs. No one need have the least fear of any discoveries that the archæologists may make, for if it should be found that there were early civilizations thousands of years before Christ it would not come into any conflict whatever with what the Bible really teaches about the antiquity of man, the Adamic race.

# VI

## Where Did Cain Get His Wife?

In almost every place that I have visited in going around the world I have given sceptics and others an opportunity of asking questions at one or two meetings. I do not think that I have ever held a question meeting at which someone has not put in the question: "Where did Cain get his wife?" This seems to be a favorite question with unbelievers of a certain class. I have also met young Christians who have been greatly puzzled and perplexed over this question. But if one will study his Bible carefully and note exactly what it says, there is really

## No Great Difficulty in the Question.

Unbelievers constantly assert that the Bible says that "Cain went into the land of Nod and took to himself a wife." In point of fact, it says nothing of the kind. An unbeliever in Edinburgh came to me with the assertion that the Bible did say this, and when I told him it did not, he offered to bet me one hundred pounds that it did. What the Bible does say is that "Cain went out from the presence of the Lord, and dwelt in the land of Nod, on the east of Eden. And Cain *knew* his wife; and she conceived and bare Enoch" (Genesis 4:16, 17). What the Bible means by "knew" in such connection anyone can discover for himself by taking his concordance and looking it up. He will discover that the word "knew" used in such connection does not mean to get acquainted with, but is connected with the procreation of the species (see for example Genesis 4:1; Judges 11:39; 1 Samuel 1:19; Matthew 1:25). Cain doubtless had his wife before going to the land of Nod and took her there with him.

But who was she, and where did he get her?

In Genesis 5:3, 4 we learn that Adam in his long life of 930 years begat many sons and daughters. There can be but little doubt that Cain married one of those numerous daughters.

But someone will say: "In that case Cain married his own sister."

Yes, that was a necessity. If the whole Adamic race was to descend from a single pair, the sons and daughters must intermarry. But as the race increased, it remained no longer necessary for men to marry their own sisters, and the practice, if continued, would result in great mischief to the race. Indeed, even the intermarriage of cousins in the present day is fraught with frightful consequences. There are parts of the globe where the inhabitants have been largely shut out from intercourse with other people and the intermarriages of cousins have been frequent and the physical and mental results have been very bad. But in the dawn of human history, such intermarriage was not surrounded with these dangers. As late as the time of Abraham, that patriarch married his half-sister (Genesis 20:12). But as the race multiplied and such intermarriages became unnecessary, and as they were accompanied with great dangers, God by special commandment forbade the marriage of brother and sister, and such marriage would now be sin because of the commandment of God; but it was not sin in the dawn of the race when the only male and female inhabitants of the earth were brothers and sisters. Such marriage today would be a crime, the crime of incest, but we cannot reasonably carry back the conditions of today into the time of the dawn of human history and judge actions performed then by the conditions and laws existing today.

If we were to throw the Bible account overboard and adopt the evolutionary hypothesis as to the origin of the human race we would not relieve matters at all, for in that case our early ancestors would have been beasts, and the father and mother of the human race would be descendants of the same pair of beasts, brother and sister beasts. Take whatever theory of the origin of the human race that we may, we are driven to the conclusion that in the early history of the race, there was the necessary intermarriage of the children of the same pair.

To sum it all up, Cain married one of the many daughters of Adam and Eve, and the impenetrable mystery that some fancy surrounds the question of where Cain got his wife is found to be no mystery whatever.

## VII

## Jehovah's Command to Abraham to Offer up Isaac as a Burnt Offering

One of the most frequent objections made to the Bible is that "the Bible says that God commanded Abraham to offer his son as a burnt offering." It is claimed that this story justifies the horrible practice of human sacrifice. Not many years ago when an insane man actually did slay his son as a sacrifice to God, infidels proclaimed far and wide that the Bible in its story of Abraham and Isaac warranted and was responsible for the action.

Not a few Christians have been bewildered and distressed by this story. How shall this apparent difficulty be removed? It can be easily met and removed in the same way that most Bible difficulties may be met and removed, namely, by noticing exactly what the Bible says and all that it says.

Notice in the first place that

### The Bible Nowhere Says

that God commanded Abraham to *slay* Isaac. It is constantly said by enemies of the Bible that God did command Abraham to slay Isaac, but this is not in reality what the Bible says. Exactly what the Bible says is that God commanded Abraham to "offer him for a burnt offering" (Genesis 22:2). Literally translated, God commanded Abraham to "make him go up [that is, upon the altar] for a burnt offering." Abraham was merely commanded to lay Isaac upon the altar as a whole offering to God. Whether when he was thus laid upon the altar and presented to God, God would require him to go further and slay his son, he did not know. All that God commanded was to make him go up on to the altar, ready to be slain and burned if God should so require. Did God so require? The record expressly declares that He did not. On the contrary, God plainly forbade the actual slaughter of Isaac (Genesis 22:11, 12). That the original command was not to kill Isaac but merely to offer him up is as plain as day from the fact that we are explicitly told that Abraham did exactly what God told him to do, that is, "to offer up Isaac." "Abraham offered up Isaac" is the Bible statement (Hebrews 11:17), but Abraham did not slay Isaac—*that* he was not told to do.

It is as clear as day, then, that the divine commandment to offer up was

## NOT A COMMAND TO SLAY.

The story as told in the Bible is not that God had first commanded Abraham to slay and burn Isaac and that He afterwards when He saw that Abraham was willing to do even this He took it back and provided a lamb to take Isaac's place. The Bible story is that God commanded Abraham to make his son Isaac to ascend the altar to be presented to God as a whole offering, and that Abraham actually did this which he was commanded to do. And this did not, either in God's original intention or in the execution of the command, involve the slaughter of Isaac.

This story, then, in no way justifies human sacrifice in the sense of the actual slaying of a human victim. On the contrary, the whole force of the narrative is against such sacrifice. Instead of being commanded it is explicitly forbidden. It does, however, justify the offering of ourselves to God wholly, as "a living sacrifice" (Romans 12:1). But this is not all that the story as it actually occurs in the Bible tells us. It goes on to tell us that so far from God commanding Abraham to slay his son, when Abraham was about to go beyond what was explicitly commanded, (namely, the offering of his son), and to slay his son, (which was not commanded), God intervened and positively forbade it. Jehovah sent His own Angel to speak in an audible voice from heaven forbidding the shedding of Isaac's blood. "Lay not thine hand upon the lad, neither do thou anything unto him," called the Angel of Jehovah out of heaven (Genesis 22:12).

This story, then, so far from encouraging human sacrifice positively and explicitly forbids it, and that in the most solemn manner. So all our difficulty with this narrative disappears when we look carefully with open eyes at the record and note precisely what is said.

## VIII

### GOD HARDENING PHARAOH'S HEART

THE various statements that are made in the Scriptures in regard to God hardening Pharaoh's heart have also perplexed a great many young Christians and have frequently been made use of by unbelievers in their attacks upon the Bible. It is said that if God hardened Pharaoh's heart and in consequence of this hardening Pharaoh rebelled against God, then God Himself was responsible for Pharaoh's sin, and that it was unjust to hold Pharaoh accountable for his rebellion and to punish him for it.

In Exodus 4:21, R. V., we read: "And the Lord said unto Moses, When thou goest back into Egypt, see that thou do before Pharaoh all the wonders which I have put in thy hand: but I will harden his heart, and he will not let the people go." See also Exodus 7:3; 14:4.

Now from reading these passages it does seem at the first glance as if there were some ground for criticism of God's action in this matter, or of the Bible account of it. But when we study carefully exactly what the Bible says, and exactly what God is reported as saying, and the circumstances under which He said it, the difficulty all disappears. For God to take a man who really desires to know and do His will, harden his heart and thus incline him not to do His will, would indeed be an action on God's part that it would be difficult or impossible to justify. But when we read God's utterances on this matter in their setting, we find this is not at all what God did with Pharaoh. Pharaoh was not a man who wished to obey God. The whole account begins—not with God's hardening Pharaoh's heart but with Pharaoh's hardening his own heart.

In Exodus 4:21 we have a prophecy of what God would do with Pharaoh, a prophecy that God made fully knowing beforehand what Pharaoh would do before He hardened his heart.

In Exodus 9:12 and later passages we have the fulfilment of this prophecy, but before God does here harden Pharaoh's heart we have a description of what Pharaoh himself did.

In Exodus 5:1, 2 we are told that Moses and Aaron appeared in the presence of Pharaoh with Jehovah's message: "Thus saith the Lord God of Israel, Let my people go, that they may hold a feast unto Me in the wilderness," and that then Pharaoh replied: "Who is the Lord that I should obey His voice to let Israel go? I know not the Lord, neither will I let Israel go." Here Pharaoh definitely and defiantly refused to recognize or obey God. This was before God hardened his heart.

## He Here Hardened His Own Heart.

Then follows a description of how Pharaoh gave himself over to more cruel oppression of the Israelites than ever (Exodus 5:3-9).

In Exodus 7:10 and following verses we see Moses and Aaron coming into the presence of Pharaoh and doing signs before him as proof that they were messengers sent from God, but Pharaoh would not listen. In the 13th verse we read in the Authorized Version: "And he hardened Pharaoh's heart, that he hearkened not unto them," but the Revised Version correctly renders: "Pharaoh's heart was hardened." It does not say as yet that the Lord hardened his heart.

The facts, then, in the case are these, that Pharaoh was a cruel and oppressive tyrant, subjecting the people of Israel to most awful bondage, suffering and death. God looked down upon His people, heard their cries, and in His mercy determined to deliver them (Exodus 2:25; 3:7, 8). He sent Moses, as His representative, to Pharaoh to demand the deliverance of His people, and Pharaoh in proud rebellion defied Him and gave himself up to even more cruel oppression of the people. It was then and only then that God hardened his heart.

This was simply in pursuance of

## God's Universal Method

of dealing with men. God's universal method is, if man chooses error, to give them up to error ( 2 Thessalonians 2:9-12, R. V.); if with a stout heart they choose sin, at last He gives them over to sin (Romans 1:24-26, 28, R. V.). This is stern dealing, but it is just dealing.

If there is any difficulty that still remains in the incident, it all disappears when we consider the manner in which God hardened Pharaoh's heart. It was, of course, not a physical act. God was not dealing with Pharaoh's heart as a part of his body. He was dealing with Pharaoh's heart in the sense in which we constantly use the word as the supposed seat of intelligence, affection and will. The will cannot be co-erced by force. The will can no more be moved by force than a train of cars can be drawn by an argument or an in-ference. The way in which God hardened Pharaoh's heart was by sending to him a series of demonstrations of His own existence and power, and a series of judgments. If Pharaoh had taken the right attitude toward these revelations of God's existence and power in these judgments that God sent upon him, they would have

## Led to His Repentance and Salvation.

But by willingly and wilfully taking the wrong attitude to-ward them, he was hardened by them. There is nothing that God sends us which is more merciful than the judgments which He sends upon our sins. If we take these judgments aright they will soften our hearts and lead us to repentance and entire surrender to God, and thus bring us salvation. But if we rebel against them, they will harden our hearts and bring us eternal ruin. The fault is not with God, and the fault is not with His judgments; the fault is with our-selves and the attitude we take toward His judgments and toward the truth of God itself. The Gospel is the savor of life unto life unto men who receive it aright, but it is the savor of death unto death to those who reject it (compare 2 Corinthians 2:15, 16). The trouble is not with the Gospel, which is "the power of God unto salvation to every one that believeth" (Romans 1:16). The trouble is with the man who rejects the Gospel, and who is thus hardened, condemned and destroyed by it, and to him it thus becomes the savor of death unto death. The same sermon brings life to one man and death to another. It brings life, pardon, and peace to the one who believes it and acts upon it. It brings condemnation and death to the one that rejects its truth. It softens the heart of one, it hardens the heart of the other. Jesus Christ Himself came into the world, not to condemn the world but to save the world (John 3:17), but to the one who believes not He brings condemnation and eternal ruin (John 3:18, 36; Hebrews 10:28, 29).

# IX

## The Wholesale Slaughter of the Canaanites by God's Command

THERE are few things in the Bible over which more intelligent readers have stumbled, and over which infidels have more frequently gloated and gloried, than God's command that certain people should be utterly exterminated, sparing neither sex nor age. Men, women and children were to be slain. Thus, for example, we read in Deuteronomy 20:16, 17 this command of God to the people of Israel: "But of the cities of these people, which the Lord thy God doth give thee for an inheritance, thou shalt *save alive nothing that breatheth*, but thou shalt utterly destroy them; namely, the Hittites, and the Amorites, the Canaanites, and the Perizzites, the Hivites, and the Jebusites; as Jehovah thy God hath commanded thee" (R. V.). In regard to other cities, it was commanded that if they sued for peace, peace was to be granted and all the inhabitants spared, but if they made war, the adult males were to be slain but the women and children were to be spared (Deuteronomy 20:10-15). These were the cities that were far away, but the inhabitants of the cities of the lands that the Israelites themselves were to inhabit were to be utterly exterminated.

We are asked: "How can we reconcile any such appallingly harsh commands as these with the doctrine so plainly taught in the New Testament that 'God is love'?" It is said that these commands can certainly not have been from God, and that the Old Testament is certainly wrong when it says that they were from God. What shall we say in reply to this?

1. First of all, let us say that it is certainly appalling that any people should be utterly put to the sword, not only the men of war, but the old men and old women as well, and the young women and the children.

But there is

## SOMETHING EVEN MORE APPALLING

than this, when one stops to think about the matter, and that is that the iniquity of any people should have become so full, their rebellion against God so strong and so universal, their moral corruption and debasement so utter and so pervasive, even down to babes just born, as to make such treatment absolutely necessary in the interests of humanity. But this was precisely the case with the nations in question. Not from the Bible alone do we learn how unfathomable were the depths of moral pollution to which these nations had sunken. They had become a moral cancer threatening the very life of the whole human race. That cancer must be cut out in every fibre if the body was to be saved. Cutting out a cancer is a dreadful operation, an operation from which any kind-hearted surgeon must shrink, but oftentimes the cutting out of the cancer is the kindest thing the surgeon can do under existing circumstances, and

## THE KINDEST THING THAT GOD COULD DO

for the human race was to cut out this cancer in every root and every fibre.

2. Let us say, in the second place, that God certainly has a right to visit judgment upon individuals and upon nations sunk in sin.

The only wonder is, when one stops to think of it, that He is so long-suffering, and that He does not visit judgment upon individuals and upon nations sooner. When one really comes to understand His holiness on the one hand, and what are the depths of covetousness, greed, lust and sin, vileness, lawlessness and contempt for God to which certain cities even today have sunken, and how young the children go astray into unmentionable vileness, one sometimes almost wonders

why He does not blot them out as He commanded the Israelites to do with the Canaanites of old! The command to ex-
terminate the Canaanites was a command big with mercy and
love. It was mercy and love, first of all, to the Israelites.
Unless the Canaanites were exterminated, they would themselves be exterminated. In point of fact, they were contami-
nated for the very reason that they did not carry out God's
stern decree to its fullest extent. They stopped short of what
God commanded them to do, and

### Stopped Short to Their Own Lasting Loss.

But what about the women—might not they be spared?
The answer is very plain. The women were the prime
source of contamination (Numbers 31:15, 16). Though true
women are nobler than true men, depraved women are more
dangerous than depraved men.

But what about the children? Might not they be spared?
Anyone who has had experience with the children of the
depraved knows how persistently the vices bred for generations in the ancestors reappear in the children even when
they are taken away from their evil surroundings and brought
up in the most favorable environment. By the regenerating
power of the Gospel it is possible to correct all this, but we
must remember that the case with which we have to deal
was centuries before the Gospel proclamation.

Love and mercy for Israel demanded just what God commanded. Love and mercy for the whole race demanded it.
God's purpose in Israel was not merely to bless Israel.
Through Israel He planned to bless the whole race. He was
training a people in the seclusion of centuries in order that
when the training was completed they might come out of the
cloister and carry benediction, salvation and life to all nations.

3. Let it be said, in the third place, that God's plans are
not only beneficent but vast, and

### It Takes Centuries to Work Them Out,

and we creatures of a day, in our little conceit, look at some little fragment of God's infinite plan and presume to judge the whole, of which we know little or nothing.

It would be well if we could only learn that God is infinite and we infinitesimal, and so of scientific and philosophic necessity His judgments are unsearchable and His ways past tracing out (Romans 11:33). A child never appears a greater fool than when criticising a philosopher, and a philosopher never appears a greater fool than when criticising God.

4. Let it be said, in the fourth place, that the extermination of the Canaanite children was not only an act of mercy and love to the world at large, it was also an act of love and mercy to the children themselves.

What awaited these children, if they were allowed to live, was something vastly worse than death. What awaited them in death it is impossible to be dogmatic about, but unless one accepts the wholly unBiblical and improbable doctrine of the damnation of all unbaptized infants we need have no fears. Even today I could almost wish that all the babes born in the slums might be slain in infancy, were it not for the hope that the church of Christ would awake and carry to them the saving Gospel of the Son of God.

5. But someone may still say: "Yes, I can see it was an act of mercy to blot out people so fallen, but why was it not done by pestilence or famine, and not by the slaying hand of the Israelites?"

The answer to this question is very simple. The Israelites themselves were in training. They were constantly falling into sin and they needed the solemn lesson that would come to them through their being made the executioners of God's wrath against the wickedness and vileness of the Canaanites. A deep impression of God's holiness and hatred of sin would thus be produced. They were distinctly told before they car-

4

ried into execution God's judgment upon the Canaanites that the reason why they were to utterly destroy the Canaanites was "tnat they teach you not to do after all their abominations which they have done unto their gods" (Deuteronomy 20:18). The whole proceeding is an impressive illustration of

### The Exceeding Hatefulness of Sin

in God's sight. It says to us that sin persisted in is a thing so grievous and ruinous as to necessitate the utter destruction of the entire race, male and female, young and old, that persists in it. It is simply the lesson that the whole Bible teaches, and that all history teaches, written in characters of fire: "The wages of sin is death."

6. Let it be said, in the next place, that those who regard sin lightly and who have no adequate conception of God's holiness will always find insurmountable difficulty in this command of God, but those who have come to see the awfulness of sin and have learned to hate it with the infinite hate it deserves, and who have caught some glimpses of the infinite holiness of God and have been made in some measure partakers of that holiness, will, after mature reflection, have no difficulty whatever with this command. It is consciousness of sin in our own hearts and lives that makes us rebel against God's stern dealings with sin.

7. There is one thing more that needs to be said. The sneering objection is sometimes made by infidels to the sparing, in certain cases, of the women as recorded in Deuteronomy 20:10-15, and also the sparing of the women in Numbers 31:21-35, 40, that the women were to be spared for immoral purposes. Thus one writer asks: "Am I to understand that God approved of taking as tribute in spoils of war, a number of virgins *for a use that is only too obvious?*" Words of similar import are to be found in a number of infidel books.

Of course, what the questioner means to imply is that these women were taken for immoral purposes. This is the use meant which is "only too obvious" to the objector. But this is not at all obvious to any pure-minded man who reads the actual Scripture account. There is in the Scripture account not the slightest intimation that the virgins were preserved for the use suggested. To the man whose own heart is evil and impure it will always be obvious that if women are preserved alive and taken as tribute they are taken for this purpose, but this will not even occur to the pure-minded man.

The whole context of the passage in Numbers 31, which is the one most frequently cited in this connection by unbelievers, is a solemn warning against immorality of this kind. And so far from this being a suggestion that God countenances acts of impurity of this character, it shows how sternly God dealt with this impurity.

In Numbers 25:1-9 we are told how the men of Israel did give themselves up to impurity with the daughters of Moab, but how in consequence the anger of the Lord was kindled against them, and how God visited their impurity with the sternest judgment. In the very chapter in question every woman who had been guilty of impurity was slain (Numbers 31:17). And in point of actual fact, it is suggested, at least by verse 18, that it was only the female *children* who could be spared. It was certainly an act of mercy on God's part to deliver these "women children" from their evil surroundings and hand them over to Israel for training where they would be brought in contact with a pure religion and trained up to become pure women. So far, according to the record, from being handed over to the Israelites for immoral purposes they were entrusted to them for the highest purposes

## X

JOSHUA COMMANDING THE SUN TO STAND STILL

ONE of the greatest difficulties in the Bible to many a student is found in the story contained in Joshua 10:12-14: "Then spake Joshua to the Lord in the day when the Lord delivered up the Amorites before the children of Israel, and he said in the sight of Israel, Sun, stand thou still upon Gibeon; and thou, Moon, in the valley of Ajalon. And the sun stood still, and the moon stayed, until the people had avenged themselves upon their enemies. Is not this written in the book of Jasher? So the sun stood still in the midst of heaven, and hasted not to go down about a whole day. And there was no day like that before it or after it, that the Lord hearkened unto the voice of a man: for the Lord fought for Israel."

Bishop Colenso wrote: "The miracle of Joshua is the most striking incident of Scripture and science being at variance." It is said by the destructive critics and the infidels that this story cannot possibly be true; that if the sun were to stand still in the way here recorded it would upset the whole course of nature.

Whether that statement by infidels be true or not no one can tell. It is simply a supposition. But certainly the God who made the earth and the sun and the whole universe could maintain it even if the sun stood still, or (to speak more accurately,) if the earth stood still on its axis and the sun appeared to stand still. But by a careful study of the Hebrew of the passage we find that the sun is not said to have stood still.

The command of Joshua in verse 12 rendered in the Authorized and Revised Versions: "Stand thou still," literally translated means: "Be silent" (see also R. V. mar-

gin), and the words rendered "stood still" in verse 13 literally translated mean "was silent." Nine times in the Bible
is it translated "keep silence"; five times at least, "be still";
in another passage, "held his peace"; in another, "quiet one's
self"; in another, "tarry"; in another, "wait"; and in another,
"rest." These renderings occur some thirty times, but it is
never rendered "stand still" except in this one passage. Indeed, in the very passage in which it is rendered "tarry" (1
Samuel 14:9), the words "stand still" do occur, but as the
translation of an entirely different Hebrew word. The word
translated "stayed" in verse 13 is sometimes translated "stand
still." It means literally "to stand" or "stand up," but it is
used of "tarrying" or remaining in any place, state or condition, as, for example, in 2 Kings 15:20; Genesis 45:1. So,
then, what the sun and moon are said to have done in the
passage is to have *tarried*, tarried from disappearing, not that
they stood absolutely still, but that their apparent motion (or
their disappearance) was

### Slowed Up or Delayed.

Furthermore, the Hebrew words translated "in the midst
of heaven" mean literally "in the half of heaven." The word
translated "midst" in considerably more than one hundred
cases is translated "half." In only five or six cases is it rendered "midst," and in one of these cases (Daniel 9:27) the
Revisers have changed "midst" to "half." In the remaining
cases, it would be as well or better "half." (For example,
Psalm 102:24.) What Joshua then bade the sun to do was to

### Linger in the Half of the Heavens,

and that is what the sun is recorded as doing. There are
two halves to the heavens, the half that is visible to us and
the other half visible on the other side of the globe.

The Hebrew preposition rendered "about" means primarily
"as" or "so."

So put these facts together, and what the story tells us is that the sun continued or tarried above the visible horizon "as a whole day." Apparently this means that an event occurred on this day near Gibeon, in the valley of Ajalon, that occurs many days every year at the North Pole, namely, that the sun remained visible for the entire twenty-four hours.

## THE METHOD

by which this was accomplished we are not told. It might be by a slight dip of the pole, or possibly by a refraction of the rays of light, or in other ways that we cannot conjecture. It certainly would not necessitate such a crash in the physical universe as objectors have imagined.

As to whether such a thing happened or not is a question of history. The history that we have reason to suppose is authentic in the Book of Joshua says that it did. It is a remarkable fact that we have a suggestion of the same thing in

## HISTORY OUTSIDE THE BIBLE.

Herodotus, the great Greek historian, tells us that the priests of Egypt showed him a record of a long day. The Chinese writings state that there was such a day in the reign of their emperor Yeo, who is supposed to have been a contemporary of Joshua. The Mexicans also have a record that the sun stood still for one entire day in the year which is supposed to correspond with the exact year in which Joshua was warring in Palestine. There is nothing of real weight to prove that there was no such day. So, upon careful examination, this which is asserted to be "the most striking incident of Scripture and science being at variance" is found to be in no sense whatever an incident of Scripture and science, or Scripture and history, being at variance.

The theory has been advanced that the words rendered "Stand thou still," but which mean literally "Be silent," should be interpreted as meaning that Joshua commanded the sun to withhold its light, to be silent in this sense, and that what occurred on this occasion was not the prolongation of a day but a dark day, so that Joshua had the advantage of fighting practically at night, though it was really the hours of the day that ought to have been light. If this is the true interpretation of "Stand thou still," all difficulty with the passage disappears. But while this interpretation might be admissible, it is difficult to see how some other portions of the narrative can be reconciled with this theory. And as already seen, the theory is not necessary to remove all difficulties in the passage.

In any event it was a miracle, but no one who believes in a God who is the Creator of the entire material universe, and a God who is historically proven to have raised Jesus Christ from the dead, ever stumbles at the mere fact of a miracle. We believe in a miracle-working God.

## XI

### DEBORAH'S PRAISE OF JAEL, "THE MURDERESS"

IT is frequently urged against the divine origin of the Bible that it defends and glorifies the treacherous murder of Sisera by Jael, and that any book that defends so violent and cruel and deceitful an action as this cannot have God for its author.

#### THE VERY SIMPLE ANSWER

to this objection is that the Bible does not defend or glorify the action of Jael. The Bible records the act in all its details. It also records the fact that Deborah, the prophetess who judged Israel at that time (Judges 4:4), predicted that the Lord would sell Sisera into the hand of a woman (Judges 4:9). It also records the fact that Deborah and Barak, in their joyful song of praise to the Lord after their deliverance from the cruel oppression of Sisera did say: "Blessed above women shall Jael the wife of Heber the Kenite be, blessed shall she be above women in the tent" (Judges 5:24). But it is nowhere hinted in the Bible account that Deborah and Barak were speaking by divine inspiration in this song of thanksgiving and praise. The Bible, by speaking of Deborah as a prophetess, no more endorses every action and every utterance of Deborah than it endorses every action and every utterance of Balaam, of whom it likewise speaks as a "prophet" (2 Peter 2:16). In the very passage in which it speaks of Balaam as a prophet, it speaks about his being rebuked for his iniquities. It is not the teaching of the Bible that every utterance of every prophet is the inspired Word of God. On the contrary, the Bible teaches that a prophet may tell lies (1 Kings 13:11-18).

The Bible nowhere justifies Jael's action. It records the action. It records Deborah and Barak's praise of the action, but it nowhere endorses this praise. We are under no necessity, therefore, of trying to justify all the details of Jael's conduct, nor indeed of trying to justify her conduct at all.

But on the other hand, we must not unjustly judge Jael. We cannot judge her in the light of New Testament ethics, for she lived some 1,300 years before Christ. She lived in a cruel age. Furthermore, she had to deal with a cruel oppressor who was working ruin among the people. It was a time of war, and war not conducted according to modern ideas of war, and we must judge her in the light of the conditions in which she lived. But even if her conduct were absolutely without excuse, it does not in the least affect the proven fact of the divine origin of the Bible. For that Book makes absolutely no attempt to defend her conduct. It simply describes it.

### The Sacrifice of Jephthah's Daughter

The story of Jephthah's daughter as recorded in the Bible has presented a great difficulty to many superficial students of the Bible, as well as to many critics of it. How can we possibly justify Jephthah's burning of his daughter as a sacrifice to Jehovah? we are often asked.

In reply we would say, in the first place, that we are nowhere told that Jephthah did burn his daughter. We are told that Jephthah vowed:

"Whatsoever cometh forth from the doors of my house to meet me, when I return in peace from the children of Ammon, shall surely be the Lord's, and I will offer it up for a burnt offering" (Judges 11:31).

The word translated "burnt offering" does not necessarily involve the idea of burning. There is no record that Jephthah's daughter was actually slain and burned. The passage that relates what actually was done with her is somewhat obscure, and many think that she was devoted by her father as an offering to God by her living a life of perpetual virginity (Judges 11:37-39).

But even supposing that she was actually slain and burned. as many candid Bible students believe that she was, (though the Bible does not actually say so), even in this case we are under no necessity of defending Jephthah's action any more than we are of defending any other wrong action of all the imperfect instruments that God, in His wondrous grace and condescension, has seen fit to use to defend or help His people. The Bible itself nowhere defends Jephthah's action. If Jephthah really did slay his daughter, he simply made a rash vow without any command or other warrant from God for so doing, and having made this rash vow he went further in his wrong doing and carried that rash vow into execution.

So the whole story instead of being a warrant for human sacrifice is intended to be a lesson upon the exceeding folly of hasty vows made in the energy of the flesh.

## "Impure" Bible Stories

An old and favorite objection to the Bible on the part of unbelievers is that there are in it "chapters that reek with obscenity from beginning to end."

That there are chapters in the Bible which describe scenes that cannot be wisely dealt with in a mixed audience we have no desire to deny; but these chapters are not obscene. To speak in the plainest terms of sin, even the vilest of sins, in order to expose its loathsomeness and in order to picture man as he really is, is not obscenity. It is purity in one of its highest forms. Whether the story of sin is obscene or not depends entirely upon how it is told and for what purpose it is told. If the story is told in order to make a jest of sin, or in order to palliate or excuse sin, it is obscene. If the story is told in order to make men hate sin, to show men the hideousness of sin, to induce men to give sin as wide a berth as possible, and to show man his need of redemption, it is not obscene, it is

### Morally Wholesome.

Now, this is precisely the way in which sin is pictured in the Bible. It is true that adultery and similar offenses against purity are mentioned by name without any attempt at mincing words. Revolting deeds of this character are plainly described, and their awful results related; but everything is so told as to make one recoil from these horrid and disgusting sins. Beyond a doubt many have been kept back from the practice of these sins by the plain things the Bible has said about them. Many others who have already fallen into these sins have been led by the Bible stories to see their enormity and their frightful consequences, and have thus been led to forsake them by what the Bible says about them. I am not speculating about this, but speak from a large experience of men and women who have been tempted to these sins and have been held back by the Bible utterances regarding them, and also from a large experience with others who have already fallen and who have been lifted up and saved by the truth on these subjects contained in the Bible.

It is said: "There is much in the Bible that is not fit to read in public," and this is brought forward as if it were an argument against the Bible. But it is an exceedingly foolish argument. There are many passages in the very best and most valuable medical works that are not fit to be read in public, they are not even fit for a father to read to his children, but he would be a fool who would cut these passages out of these medical works on that account; and he is equally a fool who objects to the Bible because there are passages in it which are invaluable in their place, but which were not intended for and are not adapted to public reading. The Bible is in part a book of moral anatomy and spiritual therapeutics, and it would be a great defect in the book, in fact an indication that it was not from God, if it did not deal with these frightful facts about man as he is and with the method of healing for these

### Foul Moral Diseases.

I, for one, thank God that these passages are in the Bible. There are things that every boy and girl need to know at a comparatively early age about some forms of sin, and loathsome sin. Many a boy and girl has dropped into these forms of sin before they realized their character simply because they were not warned against them. Ignorance about them is a misfortune. I know of no better way for them to become acquainted with the effects of these sins that they need to know about than for them to read what the Bible has to say about them. Of course, boys and girls ought not to read them together, but they ought to read them.

Instead of finding fault with the Bible for these things in it, we ought to.

## PRAISE GOD FOR PUTTING THEM THERE.

For example, there are things in the first chapter of Romans that one cannot dwell upon in public address, and, as a rule at least, one will omit two verses in the public reading of this chapter, but these two verses have been of greatest value in dealing with the heathen, and they have saved many a man in so-called Christian lands from the loathsome sins that are there exposed and denounced. An infidel in one of his works challenges Christians to know if they "dare to pick up the Bible and read from the book of Genesis the fact of Onan." He seems to think that this is a conclusive argument against the Bible, but it is simply silly. It might not be wise to read this chapter in public, but a private reading of that very story has saved many a man from the practice of a like sin. Indeed, this whole chapter, which is a favorite point of attack with infidels, has been greatly used in exposing lust and its appalling consequences.

Again, it has been said by an objector to the Bible: "Part of the holy writings consist of history and the narration of facts of a kind that cannot be mentioned in the presence of a virtuous woman without exciting horror; and should a woman be permitted to read in her chamber what she would tremble to hear at her domestic board?"

This, too, is considered a logical argument against the Bible. When one looks carefully at it and considers it, it is seen to be utter folly. Most assuredly a woman should be permitted to read in her chamber what she would tremble to hear at her domestic board. Every wise woman does it. I know of books that it would be most desirable for every woman to read in her private chamber, which if they were read at the domestic board would cause her to wish to rise from the table and leave the room with cheeks burning with shame. There are many things that men and women ought to think about, and must think about, in private that they would not for a moment discuss in public. There are books on the proper conduct of women in certain most sacred relations of life, relations of life which are as holy as any, and which can be entered into in the presence of a holy God with no question of His approval, but which do not permit of public mention. It is passing strange that intelligent men and women should use arguments so childish as this.

That the Bible is a pure book is evidenced by the fact that it is

### Not a Favorite Book in Dens of Infamy.

On the other hand, books that try to make out that the Bible is an obscene book and that endeavor to keep people from reading it are favorite books in dens of infamy. The unclean classes, both men and women, were devoted admirers of the most brilliant man this country ever produced who attacked what he called "the obscenity of the Bible." These unclean classes do not frequent Bible classes. They do frequent infidel lectures.

These infidel objectors to the book as an "obscene book" constantly betray their insincerity and hypocrisy. Colonel Ingersoll, in one passage where he dwelt upon this subject, objected to the Bible for telling these vile deeds "without a touch of humor." In other words, he did not object to telling stories of vice if only a joke was made of the sin. Thank God, that is exactly what the Bible does not do,—make a joke of sin! It makes sin hideous, so men who are

### Obscene in Their Own Hearts

object to the Bible as being an obscene book.

Some of those who make the most of the so-called "obscenity of the Book" are themselves notorious as tellers of obscene stories.

One of the men who led the attack on the Bible on the ground of its obscenity was retained by the publishers of obscene literature to defend their case.

Another man, who was a leader in his city in sending out attacks upon the Bible, challenging Christians to read in public certain portions of Scripture that were said to be immoral, was shortly afterwards found dead by his own hand in a Boston hotel side by side with a young woman who was not his wife.

A man who says: "I protest against the Bible being placed in the hands of the young because its pages reek with filth," and who does not wish people to read these "vile portions" of Scripture lest their minds be defiled, takes care to give a catalogue of the passages that he does not wish read and asks his readers to "look them up." Can anything exceed the hypocrisy of that?

I found in one city where I was holding meetings that a man who would interrupt a service by calling out about portions of the Scripture that he regarded as improper and immoral, had himself been arrested and convicted for publishing obscene literature. The truth is, these men hate the Bible. They hate it because it denounces sin and makes them uneasy in sin.

To sum it all up, there are in the Bible descriptions of sins that cannot wisely be read in every public assembly, but these descriptions of sin are morally most wholesome in the places where God, the Author of the Book, manifestly intends them to be read. The child who is brought up to read the Bible as a whole, from Genesis to Revelation, will come to know in the very best way possible what a child ought to know very early in life if he is to be safeguarded against the perils that surround our modern life on every hand. A child who is brought up upon a constant, thorough, continuous reading of the whole Bible is more likely than any other child to be free from the vices that are undermining the mental, moral, and physical strength of our boys and girls, young men and young women. But the child who is brought up on infidel literature and conversation is the easiest prey that there is for the seducer and procuress. The next easiest is the one who, through neglect of the Bible, is left in ignorance of the awful pitfalls of life.

# XIV

## David's Sin

In 2 Samuel, 11th chapter, we read the story of one of the saddest downfalls of a man of God recorded anywhere in history, and at the same time we read the record of one of the most contemptible and outrageous sins that any man ever committed against a faithful friend. We read how David committed against his faithful servant, Uriah, one of the most outrageous offenses that one man can commit against another, and how in order to cover up his sin he stained his hands with the blood of this faithful servant. After the deed was done, God in His great mercy sent His prophet to David, declaring to him: "By this deed thou hast given great occasion to the enemies of the Lord to blaspheme" (2 Samuel 12:14). History has proven the truth of this declaration. There is scarcely anything in the Bible that has caused more of the enemies of the Lord to blaspheme than this dastardly crime of king David. The enemies of the Lord are constantly bringing it up and making it the butt of pitiless ridicule.

Some who desire to defend the Bible have thought it necessary to defend David's action, or at least to try to make it appear that it was not as heinous as it looks at the first sight. But why should we seek to defend David's action? The Bible nowhere seeks to defend it. On the contrary,

## God Rebuked It

in the sternest terms. It was punished by a train of such frightful calamities as have seldom overtaken any other man.

It is true that David is spoken of in the Scriptures as "a man after God's own heart" (1 Samuel 13:14; Acts 13:22), but this does not mean by any means that David was an absolutely faultless man. It simply means that in distinction from Saul, who was constantly disposed to go his own way, David was a man who sought in all things to know God's will and to do it exactly. Therefore, he was a man after God's own heart, but though this was the abiding attitude of David's mind and heart toward God, it was still possible for him, as it is possible for men today whose wills on the whole are entirely surrendered to God, to step out of their position of absolute surrender to God and in a moment of weakness and folly to commit an act hideous in the sight of God, that will bring upon the one who commits it His sternest judgment.

The recording of David's sin without any attempt to extenuate it in the Scripture is one of the many

## PROOFS OF THE DIVINE ORIGIN

and absolute reliability of the Bible. David was the great hero of his times. Unless his Bible biographers had been guided by the Holy Spirit, they certainly would have concealed or at least have sought to palliate this awful fault of David, but in point of fact they did nothing of the kind. The Holy Spirit, who guided them in their record, led them to picture this event in all its hideousness, just as it is. Here is a radical difference between Bible biographers and all other biographers. Even the heroes of the Bible, when they fall, are not whitewashed. No excuses are offered for their sins. Their sins are not concealed from the public eye. They are recorded with fulness of detail, and the sinner is held up as a warning to others.

In this matter David "despised the word of the Lord to do that which was evil in His sight," and the Bible plainly says so (2 Samuel 12:9, 10 R. V.). "The thing that David had done displeased the Lord" (2 Samuel 11:27), and God sets him forth before the whole world as an adulterer and a murderer (2 Samuel 12:9). The whole story is too horrible for public recital, but if one will read it in private with earnest prayer he may find exceedingly precious lessons in it. It was one of the most dastardly and horrible crimes of history, but I am glad that it is recorded in the Bible. The record of it and its consequences has held many back from contemplated sin.

The story of David's sin abounds in

### GREAT LESSONS.

The first is that an exceptionally good man, yes, a man "after God's own heart," if he gets his eyes off from God and His Word, may easily fall into very gross sin. Any man who trusts in his own heart is a fool. Any man who fancies that he is a match for the devil in his own wisdom and strength is badly deceived. David was one of the noblest men of his day. He was brave, he was generous, he had a single-hearted purpose to do the will of God, but he allowed himself to trifle with temptation, and he went down to the deepest depths of vileness, baseness and dishonor.

The story also teaches that God never looks upon any man's sin with the least degree of allowance. God has no favorites, in the sense that He allows some men's sins to go unpunished. God loved David. He had given David remarkable proofs of His love, but when David sinned, God dealt with David's sin with the sternest and most relentless judgment. He allowed David's sin to dog him and to embitter and to blast his life to his dying day. God forgave David's sin and restored him to fellowship and the joy of his salvation, but He let David drink deeply of the bitter cup he had mixed for himself. One of his sons followed him into adultery, and that an adultery the burden of which came upon David's own daughter. Another son followed him into murder, and as David had rebelled against his heavenly Father, his own son rebelled against him. David was left to

### REAP WHAT HE SOWED.

When he cried over this rebellious son as he lay before him

silent in death: "O my son Absalom! my son, my son Absalom! would God I had died for thee, O Absalom, my son, my son!" (2 Samuel 18:33), David knew full well that Absalom's wandering and Absalom's death were simply the fruit of his own sin.

But there is another precious lesson for us, too, in the history of David's sin, and it is that there is full and free pardon for the vilest sinner. David's sin was black, black as midnight, it was appalling, it was inexcusable, but he found pardon full and free. David said: "I have sinned against the Lord," and God said through His prophet: "The Lord also hath put away thy sin" (2 Samuel 12:13). David himself has told us in one of his most beautiful psalms the story of his pardon (Psalm 32:1-5).

God is a holy God. He hates sin with infinite hatred. He will not look upon the smallest sin with the least bit of allowance, but God is also

## A God of Pardoning Love.

He stands ready to pardon the vilest sinner. He is ever calling to men and women who have sinned: "Let the wicked forsake his way, and the unrighteous man his thoughts, and let him return unto the Lord, for He will have mercy upon him, and to our God, for He will abundantly pardon" (Isaiah 55:7). There are those that think they have sinned too deeply to ever find pardon, but it is not so. It would be hard to find one who had sinned more deeply than David. He had committed the greatest wrong one man can commit against another, and he had stained his hands with the blood of his victim, still he found pardon.

I do thank God for this story of David. It gives me hope for any man. In the light of it as told in the Bible, I care not who comes and asks me:

"Is there salvation for me?"

I hesitate not to answer: "Yes, for you. David found mercy and you can."

## XV

## THE IMPRECATORY PSALMS

A FREQUENT objection urged against the Bible is founded upon some of the utterances in the so-called "Imprecatory Psalms." Many of these utterances have greatly perplexed earnest-minded Christians who have carefully studied the New Testament teaching regarding the forgiveness of enemies.

Three passages in the Psalms are especially cited by a recent writer as showing that the Bible is not the Word of God. These are Psalm 58:6: "Break their teeth, O God, in their mouth." It is said that this utterance exhibits so much vindictive passion that it could not possibly have been written under the inspiration of the Holy Spirit. The second passage objected to is Psalm 109:10: "Let his children be continually vagabonds, and beg: let them seek their bread also out of their desolate places." The third passage is Psalm 137:8, 9: "O daughter of Babylon, who art to be destroyed, happy shall he be that rewardeth thee as thou hast served us. Happy shall he be that taketh and dasheth thy little ones against the stones."

What shall we say about these passages?

The first thing we have to say is what we have already said in Chapter 2, namely, that God oftentimes simply records what others said—bad men, good men, inspired men and uninspired men. In the Psalms we have sometimes what God said to man, and that is always true; and on the other hand we often have what men said to God, and that may or may not be true. All of the passages cited are what men said to God. They are the inspired record of men's prayers to God. To God they breathed out the agony of their hearts, and to God they cried for vengeance upon their enemies.

Judged even by Christian standards, this was far better than taking vengeance into their own hands. Indeed, this is exactly what the New Testament commands us to do regarding those who wrong us. Vengeance belongs to God, and He will repay (Romans 12:19), and instead of taking vengeance into our own hands we should put it in His hands.

There is certainly nothing wrong in asking God to break the teeth of wicked men who are using those teeth to tear the upright. This prayer is taken from a psalm that there is every reason to suppose is Davidic, as is also the second passage quoted. But it is a well-known fact that David in his personal dealings with his enemies was most generous, for when he had his bitterest and most dangerous enemy in his hand, an enemy who persistently sought his life, he not only refused to kill him, but refused to let another kill him (1 Samuel 26:5-9). And even when he did so small a thing to Saul as to cut off the skirt of his robe, his heart smote him even for that slight indignity offered to his bitterest and most implacable enemy (1 Samuel 24:5).

## How Much Better We Would Be

if instead of taking vengeance into our own hands we would breathe out the bitterness of our hearts to God and then treat our enemies in actual fact as generously as David did! While David prayed to Jehovah in Psalm 109:10: "Let his children be continually vagabonds and beg: let them seek their bread also out of their desolate places," in point of fact, when he was in a place of power, he asked: "Is there yet any that is left of the house of Saul, that I may show him kindness?" He found a grandson of Saul's and had him eat at the king's table as one of his own sons (2 Samuel 9:1, 2, 11).

The utterance in Psalm 137:8, 9 does sound very cruel, but the utterance is a prophecy rather than a prayer. It is the declaration of awful judgment that will come upon Babylon because of the way in which Babylon had treated the people of God. Babylon was to reap what it had sown. They were to be served by others as they had served the people of God. It was a literal prophecy of what actually occurred afterwards in Babylon. We find a similar but even more awful prophecy of the coming doom of Babylon in Isaiah 13:15-18.

So when we study these Imprecatory Psalms in the light that is thrown upon them from other passages of Scripture, all the supposed difficulties disappear, and we find that there is nothing here that is not in perfect harmony with the thought that the whole Bible is God's Word, though in some instances while the record of what is said is correct and exact, that which is recorded as being said may not in itself be right; but it is God's Word that man said it, though what man said was not God's word.

## XVI

DOES THE GOD OF TRUTH AND LOVE SEND LYING SPIRITS AND
EVIL SPIRITS TO MEN?

ONE of the most puzzling passages in the Bible is found in
I Kings 22, and the parallel account in 2 Chronicles 18. In
these passages the prophet Micaiah is reported as saying:
"Therefore hear thou the word of the Lord" (v. 19, R. V.).
Then he goes on to tell: "I saw the Lord sitting on His
throne, and all the host of heaven standing by Him on His
right hand and on His left." Jehovah is pictured as asking
the assembled host who would go and persuade Ahab that
he may go up to Ramoth-gilead. Then a lying spirit is represented as coming forth and standing before the Lord, and
saying: "I will go forth and will be a lying spirit in the
mouth of all his prophets," and Jehovah is represented as
saying to the lying spirit: "Thou shalt entice him and shall
prevail." Also: "Go forth and do so" (vs. 20-22, R. V.).

At the first glance it appears here as if the Lord sanc-
tioned and took a part in lying and deception. What is the
explanation?

It is found clearly given in the context. Micaiah, speaking by the Holy Spirit, is seeking to dissuade Ahab and Jehosh-
aphat from going up to Ramoth-gilead. All the false prophets have told the two kings that they should go up to vic-
tory. Micaiah, the messenger of the Lord, tells them on the
contrary that they shall go up to defeat and to the certain
death of Ahab. He tells them that the spirit that had spoken
by the false prophets was a lying spirit. He puts this in a
highly pictorial way. But though the picture is exceedingly
vivid, it does not teach error, but truth, and teaches it in a
most forcible way, namely, that it was a lying spirit that
was in the mouth of the false prophets. But that Jehovah
was not really a party to the deception appears clearly in

71

the narrative, if we take it as a whole. So far from being
a party to the deception, He sends His own prophet to warn
them that the spirit that spoke by the false prophets was a
lying spirit, and to tell them the exact facts in the case as
to what the issue of the battle would be. If they would
choose to listen to God and His prophet they would be saved
from calamity, but if they would not listen to God and His
prophet then God would give them over to the working of
error, that they should believe a lie; but He would not do
this without abundant warning. This is

### God's Universal Method,

not only as taught in the Bible but as taught in experience,
that He gives to every man to choose either to listen to Him
and know the truth, or to turn a deaf ear to Him and to be
given over to strong delusion. If men will not receive the
love of the truth that they may be saved, then God gives
them over to strong delusion to believe a lie. If men want
lies, God gives them their fill of them (2 Thessalonians
2:10-12, R. V.).

In other passages of the Bible it seems to be taught that
God sends evil spirits to men, and the question arises: How
can we believe that a good God, a God of love, sends evil
spirits to men? Let us turn to a passage in which this is
taught, and we will soon find an answer to the difficulty.

In 1 Samuel 16:14, R. V., we read: "Now the Spirit of the
Lord had departed from Saul, and *an evil spirit* from the Lord
troubled him."

What is meant by "an evil spirit"? The context clearly
shows. It was a spirit of discontent, unrest, depression.

The circumstances were these: Saul had proved untrue to
God. He had deliberately disobeyed God (1 Samuel 15:4-35,
especially vs. 22, 23), and consequently God had withdrawn
His Spirit from him, and a spirit of discontent and unrest
had come upon him.

This was

### NOT AN UNKIND ACT ON GOD'S PART.

There was nothing kinder that God could have done. It is one of the most merciful provisions of our heavenly Father that when we disobey Him and wander from Him He makes us unhappy, discontented in our sin. If God should leave us to continue to be happy in sin, it would be the unkindest thing He could do, but God in His great mercy will win every sinner possible back to Himself, and if we sin God for our highest good sends to us deep depression and unrest in our sin. If we make the right use of this spirit of unrest and depression that God sends us, it brings us back to God and to the joy of the Holy Ghost. Saul made the wrong use of it. Instead of allowing his unrest of heart to bring him to repentance and back to God, he allowed it to embitter his soul against one whom God favored. The sending of the evil spirit was an act of mercy on God's part. The misuse of this act of mercy resulted in Saul's utter undoing.

There is many a man today who once knew something about the Spirit of the Lord and the joy of the Holy Ghost, who has fallen into sin, and God in His great love and mercy is sending him at the present time an evil spirit, a spirit of unrest, dissatisfaction, deep discontent, or even of abject misery. Let him thank God for it! Let him inquire humbly on his face before God wherein it is he has sinned against God and lost the joy of his salvation! Let him put away and confess his sin and come back to God and have renewed unto him the joy of God's salvation! An evil spirit of unrest and discontent was sent to David, too, when he sinned; but when after some resistance David confessed his sin unto the Lord, the Lord blotted it out and brought him into a place of glad joy in the Lord, where he could instruct and teach others in the way they should go (Psalm 32:4-8; 51:9-13).

## XVII

## Jonah and "the Whale."

THE story of Jonah and "the whale" has for many years been the favorite butt of ridicule with unbelievers, and the cause of not a little perplexity with those who are "unlearned and unstable." The story is quite generally discredited by the destructive critics as to its being actually historical. They attempt to explain it as allegory or parable. Those who desire to discredit the full inspiration and absolute veracity of the Bible have again and again assured us with a great show of scientific knowledge that such is the structure of a whale's mouth and the configuration of his throat that it would be impossible for a full-grown man either to pass through the sieve in its mouth or the narrow orifice of its throat, to say nothing of his coming out again alive and whole.

What shall we say to all this?

First of all, let us notice the fact that

### The Bible Nowhere Says

that Jonah was swallowed by a whale. In Jonah 1:17 we are told that Jehovah "prepared a great fish to swallow up Jonah, and Jonah was in the belly of the fish three days and three nights." There is no mention here whatever of this great fish being "a whale," with its peculiarly constructed mouth and throat. It may have been either a fish altogether prepared for the occasion, or a fish already existing providentially sent around for the purpose God had in view. In Jesus' reference to this historical event in Matthew 12:40 it is true that in the Authorized Version and in the text of the Revised Version, we read that He said that Jonah was three days and three nights in "the whale's belly"; but we read in the margin of the Revised Version that the Greek of the word rendered "whale" is "sea monster." One cannot help wondering why the translators should continue to put "whale" in the text if the Greek word means "sea monster," and it certainly does. In the Septuagint translation of the book of Jonah, "a great fish" is rendered by a Greek adjective meaning "great" and by the same word that is used in Matthew 12:40 and translated "whale." The word "whale" was in the mind of the translators and not in the word spoken by Jesus, so in neither the Old Testament nor the New Testament account is it said that Jonah was swallowed by a "whale," but by a great fish or sea monster. So we see that these very "scholarly critics" have spent much labor in proving the absurdity of something God did not inspire, and which they would have known the inspired record did not say if they had been as scholarly as they supposed.

### As to What the Great Fish Was

we are not told, but it is a well-known fact that there exist or have existed until recent times in the Mediterranean Sea, where the recorded event seems to have taken place, sea monsters—that is, dog sharks—large enough to swallow a man or horse whole. In fact, it is recorded that a man fell overboard in the Mediterranean and was swallowed by one of these sea monsters, the monster was killed and the man rescued alive. A whole horse was taken out of the belly of another.

Furthermore, even if the Bible had said that the great fish was a whale, there would be no such difficulty with the narrative as has been supposed by unbelievers and the uninformed. While it is true that there are some kinds of whale whose mouths and throats are of such a formation that it would be impossible for a full-grown man to pass through, it is not true of all kinds of whales.

The well-known author, Frank Bullen, in his book, *The*

*Cruise of the Cachalot*, says that "a shark fifteen feet in length has been found in the stomach of a cachalot." He tells further that "when dying, the sperm whale always ejects the contents of its stomach." He tells of one whale that was caught and killed, "the ejected food from whose stomach was in masses of enormous size, some of them being estimated to be the size of our hatch-house, viz., 8 feet by 6 feet by 6 feet." Of course such a whale would have no difficulty in swallowing a man, so the whole objection to the Bible narrative from the standpoint that a whale could not swallow a man is not founded upon superior knowledge, but upon ignorance.

"But," someone may say, "the action of the gastric juices would kill a man within a whale, or other sea monster."

But this leaves God out of the transaction, whereas in the Bible story God is very prominent in the whole transaction. The God who made both the monster and the man and the gastric juices could quite easily control the gastric juices and preserve the man alive. We are not trying to make out that the transaction was not miraculous in any event, but those who really believe in God and have had any large experience with God have no trouble with the miraculous.

It ought to be added, moreover, that the Bible does not tell us that Jonah remained alive during the period that he was in the belly of the great fish. There are things in the narrative as recorded in the Book of Jonah that make it appear as if he did not remain alive (Jonah 2:2, 5, 6, R. V. see margin). There seems to be

A STRONG PROBABILITY THAT JONAH ACTUALLY DID DIE

and was raised from the dead. If he actually did die, this only adds one more to the resurrections recorded in the Bible and makes Jonah a still more remarkable type of Christ. To those who believe in God, there is no difficulty in believing in the resurrection if sufficiently well attested. "Why should it be thought a thing incredible with you that God should raise the dead?" There are numerous instances on record, at least of resuscitation of men and women who to all appearances had been for some days dead. The historicity of this event is endorsed by Jesus Christ Himself (Matthew 12:40). To think of it as being merely allegory or parable is to discredit the words of Jesus.

So, on careful examination of what the Scripture says, and of the facts of history, all the difficulties supposed to exist in the story of Jonah and "the whale" are found to disappear.

# XVIII

## Some Important "Contradictions" in the Bible

I AM constantly meeting men who say that the Bible is "full of contradictions." When I ask them to show me one, they reply: "It is full of them." When I press them to point out *one*, usually they have no more to say. But now and then I meet an infidel who does know enough about his Bible to point out some apparent contradictions. In this chapter we will consider some of these.

### Can Man See God?

1. One of those most frequently brought forward is the apparent contradiction between John 1:18, where we read: "No man hath seen God at any time," and Exodus 24:10, where we are told of Moses and Aaron, Nadab and Abihu and seventy of the elders of Israel that "they saw the God of Israel." (There are also other passages in which men are said to have seen God.)

Now this certainly looks like a flat contradiction, and many besides sceptics and infidels have been puzzled by it. Indeed, one of the most devout men I ever knew was so puzzled by it that he left his place of business and came miles in great perturbation of spirit to ask me about it. The solution of this apparently unanswerable difficulty is in reality very simple.

We must remember first of all that two statements which in terms flatly contradict one another may be both of them absolutely true, for the reason that the terms are not used in the same sense in the two statements.

For example, if any man should ask me if I ever saw the back of my head, I might answer: "No, I never saw the back of my head," and this statement would be strictly true.

Or I might answer: "Yes, I have seen the back of my head," and this statement would also be true, though it appears to flatly contradict the other. The back of my head I never have seen, but more than once when looking into a glass with another glass back of me I have seen the back of my head. It depends entirely upon what the man means when he asks me the question if I ever saw the back of my head what I should answer him. If he means one thing I answer "No," and that is true. If he means another thing I answer "Yes," and that is equally true.

But someone may object: "In the latter case you did not really see the back of your head. What you saw was a reflection of the back of your head in the mirror."

But to this I would reply: "Neither do you see the back of anyone's head when you are looking right at it. What you see is the reflection of that person's head upon the retina of your eye."

But every one knows what you mean when you use language in this common sense, every-day way of using it. They know that when you say you saw the back of another man's head that you mean you saw a reflection of it upon the retina of your eye, and they know when you say you saw the back of your own head in the glass that you mean that you saw the reflection of the back of your head in the glass. In the one case you see the reflection, in the other case you see the reflection of the reflection, and in both cases what you actually see is the thing that was reflected.

Now in this case before us in the Bible it is all very like this illustration. God in His eternal essence is "invisible" ("unseeable," 1 Timothy 1:17). No man hath seen Him, nor can we see Him (1 Timothy 6:16). He is spirit, not form (John 4:23, 24), so John tells us in the passage before us the profound and wondrous truth: "No man hath seen God at any time. The only begotten Son which is in the bosom of the Father, He hath declared Him." That is, this invisible (unseeable) God is unfolded to us, interpreted to us, (the word here translated "declared" is the word from which our word "exegesis" is derived), in the words and in the person of Jesus Himself. So fully is He declared, not only in the words of Jesus but in His person, that Jesus could say: "He that hath seen Me hath seen the Father" (John 14:9).

But this essentially invisible God has been pleased in His great grace to manifest Himself again and again in bodily form. Moses and the seventy elders saw such a manifestation of God (or theophany) when they were in the mount. Isaiah saw such a manifestation in the temple (Isaiah 6:1), and in describing it he properly declared: "I saw the Lord." Job saw such a manifestation and was so humbled by the actual coming face to face with God Himself in this manifestation of God, that he cried: "I abhor myself, and repent in dust and ashes" (Job 42:6). It was God that was manifested in these theophanies, and so it was God they saw.

We see then that both of these apparently flatly contradictory statements that "No man hath seen God at any time" and that "Moses [and the others] saw God" are perfectly true.

Jesus Christ Himself was the crowning manifestation of God. "In Him dwelleth all the fulness of the Godhead bodily" (that is, in bodily form, Colossians 2:9). So Jesus said to Philip with perfect propriety: "He that hath seen Me hath seen the Father." The time is coming when all the pure in heart shall behold God permanently manifested in bodily form (Matthew 5:8). The form in which Jesus existed in His pre-existent state in the glory was the form of God (Philippians 2:6, see R. V. margin). The Greek word which is translated "form" in this passage means "the form by which a person or thing strikes the vision—the external appearance" (Thayer's *Greek-English Lexicon of the New Testament*), so we are clearly taught that the external appearance of Jesus in His pre-existent form was the external appearance of God, that is, that the invisible God, who is a spirit in His essential essence, manifests Himself in an external, visible form.

## THE SUPERSCRIPTIONS ON THE CROSS.

2. A second "contradiction," of which the infidels make a great deal and by which not a few believers are puzzled, is that found in the four accounts of the superscriptions on the cross. We read in Matthew 27:37: "And set up over His head His accusation written, This is Jesus the King of the Jews." We read in Mark 15:26: "And the superscription of His accusation was written over, The King of the Jews." We read in Luke 23:38: "And there was also a superscription over Him, This is the King of the Jews" (R. V.). And we read in John 19:19: "And Pilate wrote a title, and put it on the cross. And the writing was, Jesus of Nazareth the King of the Jews." Now no two of these agree absolutely in the words used, and it is asked by the objector: "How can all four possibly be right?" It is said that at least three must be wrong, at least in part. A great deal is made of this difficulty by those who argue against the verbal inspiration of the Scriptures.

I am surprised that anyone should make so much of it, for the answer is found so plainly stated in the very passages cited that it is surprising that any careful student should have overlooked it. John tells us in John 19:20, R. V., that in order that all the different nationalities present might read it, the charge upon which Jesus was crucified was written in Hebrew, in Latin and in Greek; in Hebrew for the common people, in Latin for the Roman, and in Greek, the universal language. The substantial part of the charge was that Jesus claimed to be "the King of the Jews" and was crucified for making this claim, so these words, "The King of the Jews," appear in the Hebrew and the Latin and the Greek, and it also appears in all four accounts of the four Gospels. Matthew (writing for the Jews) would naturally give the inscription as it appeared in Hebrew, Mark (writing for the Romans) would be likely to give it as it appeared in the Latin, and Luke as it appeared in the Greek. Presumably John gives it in the full Roman form, "Jesus of Nazareth" being

6

a full and explicit statement of who Jesus was, and the charge being His claim to be "The King of the Jews."

The only thing that is left then to account for is the difference between Mark and John, but if we carefully read Mark 15:26 we see that Mark does not claim to give the full wording that appeared on the cross. He simply says: "*The superscription* of His accusation was written over." The accusation was: "The King of the Jews," and this Mark gives, and this alone. The words, "This is Jesus of Nazareth," were not the accusation, but the name of the accused.

So all this difficulty, of which so much is made, disappears altogether when we notice exactly what is said and all that is said.

## THE CONVERSION OF SAUL.

3. Another "contradiction" of which a great deal is made is that which seems to exist between two different accounts of the conversion of Saul of Tarsus. We are told in Acts 9:7 that those who journeyed with Saul to Damascus *heard the voice* that spoke to Saul, but saw no man. On the other hand Paul, in relating to the Jews in Jerusalem the story of his conversion, says: "They that were with me beheld indeed the light, but they *heard not the voice* of Him that spake to me" (Acts 22:9, R. V.) Now these two statements seem to flatly contradict one another. Luke, in recounting the conversion, says that the men that journeyed with Paul heard the voice, but Paul himself in recounting his conversion says that they heard not the voice. Could there possibly be a flatter contradiction than this?

But this apparent contradiction disappears when we look at the Greek of the two passages. The Greek word translated "heard" governs two cases, the genitive and the accusative. When a person or thing the voice of which is heard is spoken of, it is followed by the genitive. When the message that is heard is spoken of it is followed by the accusative. In Acts 9:7 the genitive is used. They did hear the voice, the sound. In Acts 22:9 the words translated "the voice" are in the accusative. They did not hear the message of the One that spoke. The word rendered "voice" also has two meanings: first, "a sound, a tone," and second, "a voice," that is, "a sound of uttered words" (Thayer's *Greek-English Lexicon of the New Testament*). The voice as a mere sound they heard; the voice as the sound of uttered words, the message, they did not hear.

So another seeming difficulty entirely disappears when we look exactly at what the Bible in the original says, and instead of having an objection to the Bible we have another illustration of its absolute accuracy, not only down to a word but down to a single letter that ends a word and by which a case is indicated.

## THE RESURRECTION OF JESUS CHRIST.

4. A good deal is made by some who deny the accuracy of the Bible of the apparent contradictions in the various accounts of the resurrection of Jesus Christ from the dead. The most prominent unbeliever in his own city sent to the daily papers the following problem for me to solve. He said: "The account of the visit to the grave is entirely different in the four Gospels. Two of the Gospels state that the women saw two angels at the grave, and two of the other Gospels state that they only saw one angel."

What is the solution of this apparent difficulty?

First of all, let it be said that the objector does not truly state the facts in the case. So far from its being true that two of the Gospels state that they "saw only one angel," not one of the Gospels states that they saw *only* one angel. It is true that Matthew says that "they saw an angel" (Matthew 28:1-5), and Mark says: "They saw a young man," presumably an angel, (Mark 16:5-7), but neither Matthew nor Mark says that they saw "only" one angel. Saying that they saw one does not preclude the possibility of their seeing two. Furthermore, let it be noticed that it is not true, as stated by the objector, that two of the Gospels state that the women saw two angels at the grave. It is true that Luke says (Luke 24:3, 4) that after they had entered into the sepulchre two men (presumably angels) stood by them in dazzling apparel. But this apparently does not refer to the incident that Matthew refers to at all, for the angel there mentioned was an angel who was outside the sepulchre. Nor does it seem to refer to the same fact of which Mark speaks, for the young man (or angel) in Mark's Gospel was one who was sitting on the right side of the sepulchre. This angel may have been joined later by the one who was on the outside, and these two together may have stood by the women. This seems the more likely, as the message uttered by the two in Luke is in part the same as that uttered by the angel outside the sepulchre in Matthew, and by the young man inside the sepulchre in Mark (compare Luke 24:5, 6 with Matthew 28:5-7; Mark 16:5-7). The very simple solution of it all is that there was an angel outside the tomb when the women approached, and they saw another one inside sitting. The one outside entered, and the one sitting arose, and standing by the women they uttered together or after one another the words recorded in Matthew and in Mark and in Luke.

But how about the account in John? John does tell us that there were two angels in white sitting, one at the head and one at the feet where the body of Jesus had lain (John 20:12, 13). How can we reconcile that with the other three? Very easily. It was not the *group of women* at all that saw these two angels, but we are distinctly told it was Mary alone. Mary started out with the other women for the sepulchre, got a little ahead of the group, was the first to see the stone rolled away from the tomb (John 20:1), immediately jumped at the conclusion that the tomb had been rifled and ran at the top of her speed to the city to carry the news to Peter and John (John 20:2). While she is going into the city, the other women reach and enter the tomb, and the things recorded in Matthew, Mark and Luke occur. These women have left the sepulchre before Mary reaches it the second time. Peter and John have also left it when Mary reaches the sepulchre, and two angels, the one who had been on the outside and the one who at first had been sitting on the inside, were both sitting, one at the head and the other at the feet where the body of Jesus had lain.

All the other apparent contradictions in the four accounts of the resurrection, and they are quite numerous, also disappear on careful study. But these apparent contradictions are themselves

### PROOF OF THE TRUTH AND THE ACCURACY

of the accounts. It is evident that these four accounts are separate and independent accounts. If four different persons had sat down to make up a story in collusion of a resurrection that never occurred, they would have made their four accounts appear to agree, at least on the surface. Whatever of contradictions there might be in the four accounts would only come out after minute and careful study. But just the opposite is the case here. It is all on the surface that the apparent contradictions occur. It is only by careful and protracted study that the real agreement shines forth. It is just such a harmony as would not exist between four accounts fabricated in collusion. It is just such an agreement as would exist in four independent accounts of substantially the same circumstances, each narrator telling the same story from his own standpoint, relating such details as impressed him, omitting other details which did not impress him but which did impress another narrator and which the other narrator related. Sometimes two accounts would seem to contradict one another, but the third account would come in and unintentionally reconcile the apparent discrepancies between the two. This is precisely what we have in the four accounts of the resurrection of Jesus Christ. We may heartily thank God that there are these apparent discrepancies among them. And even if we cannot find the solution of some apparent discrepancies, the fact that we do by careful study find a solution of

what appeared to be an inexplicable contradiction will suggest to us the certainty that if we knew all the facts in the
case, we could also find a solution of the apparent discrepancies which we cannot reconcile as yet. The more one
studies the four accounts of the resurrection, the more he
will be convinced, if he is candid, that they are separate and
independent accounts, and a truthful narration of what actually occurred. They could not have been fabricated in collusion with one another,—the very discrepancies urged prove
this. Much less could they have been fabricated independently of one another. Four men sitting down independently
of one another to fabricate an account of something that never
occurred would have agreed with one another nowhere, but
in point of fact the more we study these four accounts the
more clearly do we discover how marvellously they fit in to
one another.

What has been said about the apparent discrepancies between the four accounts of the resurrection will apply also
to other apparent discrepancies in the different Gospel narratives of the same event. They are very numerous, and to
take them all up in detail would require a volume, but the
illustration given above will serve to prove how these apparent discrepancies can be reconciled one by one if we take
them up thoroughly. And if there are any that still refuse
to yield to our hardest study, we may be confident that if
we knew all the facts in the case the apparent discrepancy
could be readily reconciled.

## DOES GOD REPENT?

5. Another apparent "contradiction" of the Scripture of
which a great deal is made and which has puzzled a great
many believers is this:

We read in Malachi 3:6: "For I am the Lord, I change
not"; and in James 1:17: "Every good gift and every perfect gift is from above, and cometh down from the Father
of lights, with whom is no variableness, neither shadow of
turning"; and I Samuel 15:29: "And also the Strength of

Israel will not lie nor repent: for He is not a man that He should repent." But in apparently flat contradiction of these we read in Jonah 3:10: "And God saw their works, that they turned from their evil way; and *God repented* of the evil that He had said that He would do unto them, and He did it not"; and in Genesis 6:6: "And *it repented the Lord* that He had made man on the earth, and it grieved Him at His heart." Here it not only says "it repented God," but "it grieved Him at His heart." Now this appears like a flat contradiction. What is the explanation?

The explanation is that what the first set of passages says is absolutely true, that God is absolutely unchangeable, He is "the same yesterday, and today and forever" (Hebrews 13:8). But the second class of passages is also true, for if God does remain the same in character, infinitely hating sin and absolutely unchangeable in His purpose to visit sin with judgment, then if any city or any person changes in attitude toward sin, God must necessarily change in His attitude toward that person or city. If God remains the same, if His attitude toward sin and righteousness is unchanging, then must His dealings with men change as they turn from sin to repentance. His character remains ever the same, but His dealings with men change as they change from the position that is hateful to His unchanging hatred of sin to one that is pleasing to His unchanging love of righteousness.

We may illustrate this by the direction of a railway station that remains stationary, relative to a train that moves along the track in front of the station. When the train begins to move it is to the east of the station (say), but as the train moves westward it is soon west of the station. The only way in which the station could maintain the same direction relative to the moving train would be by moving as the train moves. If the station is unchangeable in its position, its direction relative to the train must change as the train moves. So it is with God's attitude toward man. If God remains unchangeable in His character, His purpose and His position, then as man moves from sin to righteousness, God's attitude relative to that man must change. The very fact that God does not repent (change His mind), that He remains always the same in His attitude toward sin, makes it necessary that God should repent in His conduct (change His dealings with men) as they turn from sin to righteousness.

As to Jehovah's repenting of having made man on the earth and its grieving Him at His heart, this too is necessitated by the unchanging attitude of God toward sin. If God does not repent (change His mind about sin, His attitude toward sin), and if man's wickedness becomes great, then God's unrepenting, unchanging hatred of sin necessitates that the man whom He has created, who has fallen into sin so great and so abhorrent to Himself, should become the object of great grief to Him, and that He should turn from His creative dealings with man to His destroying dealings with man. This was necessitated by man's sin. An unchangeably holy God must destroy man who has become so hopelessly sunken in sin. The only condition upon which He could spare him would be that God Himself change from the holiness of His character as it was when He created him to become an unholy God.

So again we see that what appears at the first glimpse like a flat contradiction is really no contradiction at all but an entire agreement in fact and thought between passages that seem to contradict in words.

## WHO MOVED DAVID TO NUMBER ISRAEL?

6. Another apparent "contradiction" of Scripture that is frequently urged is found in 2 Samuel 24:1 compared with 1 Chronicles 21:1. In 2 Samuel 24:1, R. V., we read that "the anger of the Lord was kindled against Israel, and He moved David against them, saying, Go number Israel and Judah," but in 1 Chronicles 21:1 we read: "And Satan stood up against Israel and moved David to number Israel." In one passage, therefore, we are told that Jehovah moved David against the people when He said: "Go and number Israel and Judah," in the other passage we are told that Satan moved David to number Israel, and we are asked: "Which is the correct account?"

The very simple answer to this question is that both accounts are correct.

We do not need even to suppose that an error has crept into the text and that "he" appears instead of Satan, so that what really was recorded in Samuel would be: "And again the anger of the Lord was kindled against Israel, and Satan moved David against them," meaning that the anger of the Lord was kindled because he yielded to Satan's moving him. Of course it is possible that such an error may have crept into the text, or it is possible that the pronoun "he" really refers to Satan, who is not mentioned, or the "he" might be interpreted "one," without any designation as to who the "one" was. If this were so there would be no difficulty whatever in the passage.

But there is no insuperable difficulty in any case to anyone who understands the Bible teaching regarding God's relation to temptation, and the attitude that He takes toward Satan. In 2 Corinthians 12:7, R. V., we are told by Paul that lest he should be exalted above measure through the abundance of the revelations made to him there was given him a thorn in the flesh, "a messenger of Satan," to buffet him. Now as the purpose of this thorn in the flesh, this "messenger of Satan," was most salutary, to keep Paul from being "exalted overmuch," evidently it was God who gave the thorn in the flesh, the "messenger of Satan"; but none the less the messenger was a messenger of Satan. In other words, God uses Satan, evil as he is, for our good, for our moral discipline. Just as God makes the wrath of man to praise Him (Psalm 76:10), so He makes even the wrath of Satan to praise Him. What Satan intends only for evil God uses for our good. It was Satan who tempted David, but it was by God's permission that Satan tempted him, and back of the testing and consequent failure of David and the salutary humiliation of David that came out of it was God, and in this sense it was God who moved David to the act that David might discover through his failure what was in his own heart.

## XIX

## "Mistakes" in the Bible

The Bible is said not only to be full of "contradictions," but also to contain "mistakes."

1. One of the "mistakes" most constantly referred to by destructive critics is found in Matthew 27:9, 10 (R. V.): "Then was fulfilled that which was spoken by Jeremiah the prophet, saying, And they took the thirty pieces of silver, the price of Him that was valued, whom certain of the children of Israel did price, and gave them for the potter's field, as the Lord appointed me."

Now the passage here referred to by Matthew is found in the prophecy ascribed in the Old Testament to Zechariah (Zechariah 11:11-13). At first sight this appears as if Matthew had made a mistake and ascribed to Jeremiah a prophecy that was really made by Zechariah. Even John Calvin seems to have thought that Matthew made a mistake. He says:

"How the name of Jeremiah crept in I confess I do not know, nor do I give myself much trouble to inquire. The passage itself plainly shows the name of Jeremiah has been put down by mistake instead of Zechariah; for in Jeremiah we find nothing of this sort, nor anything that even approaches it."

This passage has been pressed as proof that the Gospel narratives are not necessarily "historical accounts of what actually occurred." Must we admit that Matthew was mistaken? There is not the slightest necessity of admitting that Matthew was mistaken.

In the first place, in some manuscripts the word "Jeremiah" does not appear, but the passage reads: "Then was fulfilled that which was spoken by the prophet," without any mention as to who the prophet was. In still another reading, "Zechariah" appears instead of "Jeremiah." Westcott and Hort do not accept the reading without "Jeremiah," nor the reading which substitutes "Zechariah" for "Jeremiah," but they do mention these readings, *especially the first, as* "noteworthy rejected readings." Mrs. Lewis says that some of the earliest and best manuscripts omit the word "Jeremiah." So the apparent mistake here may be due to the error of a copyist.

However, the best textual critics all accept the reading "Jeremiah" in this passage, and it seems to the writer that this is probably the correct reading. If then in the Gospel of Matthew as originally written Matthew used the word "Jeremiah" here, was it not a mistake?

Not at all necessarily. That these words or words very similar to them are found in the prophecy which in our Old Testament bears the name of Zechariah is unquestionably true, but it does not follow at all from this that Jeremiah did not speak them, for it is a well-known fact that the later prophets of the Old Testament often quoted the predictions of earlier prophets. For example, Zechariah himself in Zechariah 1:4 quoted a prophecy known to be Jeremiah's (see Jeremiah 18:11), and in the passage which we are now considering Zechariah may also have

QUOTED FROM THE PROPHECY OF JEREMIAH.

There is no record in the book of Jeremiah as we now have it in the Old Testament of Jeremiah's having uttered this prophecy, but there is no reason whatever to think we have in Jeremiah all the prophecies that Jeremiah uttered, and Zechariah may easily have had access to prophecies of Jeremiah not recorded in the book of Jeremiah.

Furthermore it is to be noted that Zechariah himself says in Zechariah 7:7: "Should ye not hear the words which the Lord hath cried by the former prophets?" so it is evident that

Zechariah regarded it as part of his mission to recall the prophecies of the prophets that had gone before him. He would be especially inclined to recall the prophecies of Jeremiah, for it was a saying among the Jews that "the spirit of Jeremiah was upon Zechariah."

So we see that this much-vaunted mistake of Matthew does not appear to have been a mistake at all when we closely examine it.

Perhaps it ought to be added that there has been much question by the critics as to whether the closing chapters of the book of Zechariah were really a portion of the prophecies of Zechariah. There is nothing in the chapters themselves to indicate that they were. It is true that for centuries they have been attached to the prophecies of Zechariah, but nowhere in the Bible does it state that they were by Zechariah, and it has been held that they were in reality not by Zechariah but by Jeremiah. This, however, is a question for the critics. If it should prove to be so, it would simply be an additional confirmation of the accuracy of Matthew's statement, but even if it is not so, if Zechariah is the author of this prophecy (Zechariah 11:11-13) as we find it in the Bible, it does not at all prove that Jeremiah may not have uttered a similar prophecy to which Zechariah referred and which Matthew has accurately quoted. And the critics will have to search farther if they wish to prove Matthew to have been in error.

## ABRAHAM'S SEPULCHRES.

2. A second alleged "mistake" in the Bible is the statement of Stephen in Acts 7:16: "And were carried over into Sychem, and laid in the sepulchre that Abraham bought for a sum of money *of the sons of Emmor*, the father of Sychem." Genesis 23:17, 18 states: "And the field of *Ephron*, which was in Machpelah, which was before Mamre, the field, and the cave which was therein, and all the trees that were in the field, that were in all the borders round about, were made sure unto

Abraham." Stephen seems, then, to have been mistaken in his statement that Abraham bought it of the sons of Emmor.

Let me put the supposed mistake in the words of a prominent doctor of divinity. He says: "According to Luke's report, Stephen says Abraham bought a sepulchre *of the sons of Emmor*, the father of Sychem (Acts 7:16). But Genesis 23:17, 18 says Abraham bought it of *Ephron the Hittite*, and Genesis 33:19 says that *Jacob* bought it of the sons of Emmor. . . . John Calvin says Stephen evidently made a mistake. Dr. Hackett admits that Stephen appears to have confounded the two transactions . . . but what do those say about it . . . who maintain the absolute inerrancy of the Bible?"

This seems like a puzzler until one notices exactly what the three passages referred to say, then the puzzle is solved. The very simple solution is as follows:

First, Genesis 23:17, 18 does not say what the objector says it does say; that is, it does not say that Abraham bought *this sepulchre to which Stephen refers* of Ephron the Hittite. It does state that Abraham bought *a field* of Ephron the Hittite, in which there was a cave, and that Abraham buried his wife Sarah in this cave. But there is no good reason for supposing that this was the sepulchre in which Jacob and the patriarchs were buried. There is no reason for supposing that Abraham in his long lifetime bought but one burial place. The writer of this book has himself purchased two, one in Chicago where his brother is buried, and one in Northfield, Mass., where his daughter is buried, and is also interested in a third in Brooklyn where his father and mother and other brother are buried. There is not the slightest hint in the Scriptures that these two sepulchres mentioned in Genesis 23:17, 18 and in Acts 7:16 are the same.

As to the passage in Genesis 33:19, where, according to the objector, it is said that Jacob, and not Abraham (as Stephen puts it), bought the sepulchre, this passage does not, in point of fact, say that Jacob bought *the sepulchre*. It says he bought *"the parcel of a field* at the hand of the children of

Hamor" (the ones of whom Stephen says Abraham bought the sepulchre). The presumption in the case is that Abraham had already purchased the sepulchre at an earlier date and that Jacob in his day purchased the ground ("a parcel of land") in which the sepulchre was located. When Abraham purchased a sepulchre to bury Sarah he took the precaution of buying the field as well as the sepulchre, but in the latter case he seems to have purchased the sepulchre without buying the whole piece of ground, which therefore Jacob himself bought at a later date. It is altogether likely that Abraham should have purchased a sepulchre in this spot in his later life, for it was a place dear to him by many memories (see Genesis 12:6, 7).

So, after all, the mistake was not Stephen's, but the mistake of the commentators who were not careful to note exactly what Stephen said and what is said in the two passages in Genesis.

Joshua informs us that it was in this parcel of ground which Jacob bought (which presumably contained the sepulchre that Abraham had bought at an earlier date) that the bones of Joseph were buried (Joshua 24:32). Apparently Stephen was a more careful student of Old Testament Scripture than some of his critics.

But even allowing for the moment that Stephen was mistaken in this case, it would prove nothing whatever against the divine origin of the Bible or its absolute inerrancy, for Stephen is not one of the authors of the Bible. He was not a prophet or an apostle. It is true he was a Spirit-filled man, but he was not the writer of a book in the Bible. The inspired author of the Acts of the Apostles records that Stephen said these words, and if these words that Stephen uttered had been mistaken, the record that he said them would still be correct. It would be God's Word that Stephen said this, but what Stephen said would not be God's word. The one who contends for the divine origin of the Bible and its absolute accuracy is under no obligation whatever to prove the accuracy of every statement that every speaker in the

Bible, even every Spirit-filled speaker, is recorded as saying (see page 20).

## THE USE OF STRONG DRINK IN PROVERBS 31:6, 7.

4. Another alleged "mistake" in the Bible is found in Proverbs 31:6, 7: "Give strong drink unto him that is ready to perish, and wine unto the bitter in soul. Let him drink and forget his poverty, and remember his misery no more" (R. V.). It is said that this advocates the use of intoxicating liquor under certain conditions, and that as the use of intoxicating liquor under any and all circumstances is wrong this teaching of the Bible is a mistake.

But the difficulty disappears, as many another difficulty will disappear, if we do not rip the verses out of their context, but study them, as any passage in any book should be studied, in the context. The whole section from verses 1 to 9 is a protest against kings (and by implication persons in any place of responsibility) using wine or strong drink at all. It is plainly taught that any use of wine has a tendency to make them forget the law and to pervert judgment. Verses 6 and 7 go on to add that wine and strong drink should only be used in cases of extreme physical weakness and despondency, when the man is so far gone that he is "ready to perish," and is consequently in the deepest depths of despondency ("bitter in soul," R. V.). The words are addressed to the king (R. V.), and the king, who was able to buy wine, instead of using it himself should give it to those who are in such physical condition that they need it. The one in this condition would be stimulated by the wine, lifted out of his depression, by the generosity of the king who gave the wine, so that he would be enabled to "forget his poverty," which would naturally preclude him from buying the wine for himself. The whole passage goes on to urge the king's attention to "the cause of the poor and needy."

So there remains no difficulty in this passage except for those who hold that the use of intoxicating liquors is wrong under *any* circumstances. But there are many who hold that in extreme cases of physical weakness the use of wine is wise and permissible.

We do not need to go into the question as to whether the wine and strong drink in this case were alcoholic. Those who urge that "strong drink" in the Old Testament often-times refers to a heavy, sweet unfermented wine have a good deal to say in favor of their position. Of course, if this inter-pretation were true, it would remove all difficulty from the passage. But in any case there is really no difficulty here at all for anyone who believes that there are circumstances in which the use of alcoholic stimulants is advisable. As there was a time in the early life of the writer of this book when the doctors had all given him up to die and when his life was sustained by a prescription of an old nurse, one of the main ingredients of the prescription being brandy, he is naturally disposed to think there are cases like that mentioned in the text when the use of strong drink is warrantable. But he thoroughly agrees with the context of the passage, which teaches that all use of wine should be renounced by people in health and strength and prosperity.

## Jesus Turning Water into Wine.

5. A stock objection against the Bible, and not only against the Bible but against Jesus Christ Himself, is found in the story of Jesus turning the water into wine at the mar-riage festival at Cana of Galilee as recorded in John 2:1-11.

But there need be no difficulty in this action of Jesus even for the extreme teetotaler if he considers carefully exactly what is said and precisely what Jesus did.

The wine provided for the marriage festivities at Cana failed. A cloud was about to fall over the joy of what is properly a festive occasion. Jesus came to the rescue. He provided wine, but there is not a hint that the wine He made was intoxicating. It was fresh-made wine. New-made wine is never intoxicating. It is not intoxicating until some time after the process of fermentation has set in. Fermentation is a process of decay. There is not a hint that our Lord produced alcohol, which is a product of decay or death. He produced a living wine uncontaminated by fermentation. It is true it was better wine than they had been drinking, but that does not show for a moment that it was more fermented than that which they had before been drinking. The writer of this book is a thorough-going teetotaler. He does not believe at all in the use of alcoholic stimulants even in cases of sickness, except in the most extreme cases, and even then only with the greatest caution, but he has not the slightest objection, and does not think that any reasonable person can have the slightest objection, to anyone's drinking new-made wine, that is, the fresh juice of the grape. It is a wholesome drink. Even if some of the guests were already drunken, or had drunk freely (see v. 10, R. V.) of wine that may have been intoxicating, there would be no harm, but good, in substituting an unintoxicating wine for the intoxicating drink which they had been taking. Our Lord, as far as this story goes at least, did not make *intoxicating* liquor for anybody to drink, but simply saved a festive occasion from disaster by providing a pure, wholesome, unintoxicating drink. By turning the water into a wholesome wine, He showed His creative power and manifested His glory.

7

# XX

## The Two Genealogies of Jesus, the Christ

A Favorite point of attack on the Bible for those who deny its divine origin and inerrancy is the two varying genealogies of Jesus Christ. Not only is this a favorite point of attack by unbelievers, but it is also a point that often puzzles earnest students of the Bible. It is perfectly clear that the two genealogies differ widely from one another, and yet each is given as the genealogy of Christ. How can they by any possibility both be true? One has recently written me on this question in these words: "Two genealogies of Jesus are given, one in Matthew and one in Luke, and one is entirely different from the other. How can both be correct?"

A very simple answer to this apparently difficult question is this:

1. The genealogy given in Matthew is the genealogy of Joseph, the reputed father of Jesus, his father in the eyes of the law. The genealogy given in Luke is the genealogy of Mary, the mother of Jesus, and is the human genealogy of Jesus Christ in actual fact. The Gospel of Matthew was written for Jews. All through it Joseph is prominent, Mary is scarcely mentioned. In Luke, on the other hand, Mary is the chief personage in the whole account of the Saviour's conception and birth. Joseph is brought in only incidentally and because he was Mary's husband. In all of this there is a deep significance.

2. In Matthew Jesus appears as the Messiah. In Luke He appears as "the Son of man," our Brother and Redeemer, who belongs to the whole race and claims kindred with all kinds and conditions of men. So in Matthew the genealogy

descends from Abraham to Joseph and Jesus, because all the predictions and promises touching the Messiah are fulfilled in Him. But in Luke the genealogy ascends from Jesus to Adam, because the genealogy is being traced back to the head of the whole race and shows the relation of the second Adam to the first.

3. Joseph's line in Matthew is the strictly royal line from David to Joseph. In Luke, though the line of descent is from David, it is not the royal line. In this Jesus is descended from David through Nathan, David's son indeed, but not in the royal line, and the list follows a line quite distinct from the royal line.

4. The Messiah, according to prediction, was to be the actual son of David according to the flesh (2 Samuel 7:12-19; Psalm 89:3, 4, 34-37; 132:11; Acts 2:30; 13:22, 23; Romans 1:3; 2 Timothy 2:8). These prophecies are fulfilled by Jesus being the son of Mary, who was a lineal descendant of David, though not in the royal line. Joseph, who was of the royal line, was not his father according to the flesh, but was his father in the eyes of the law.

5. Mary was a descendant of David through her father, Heli. It is true that Luke 3:23 says that Joseph was the son of Heli. The simple explanation of this is that Mary being a woman her name according to Jewish usage could not appear in the genealogy, males alone forming the line, so Joseph's name is introduced in the place of Mary's, he being Mary's husband. Heli was his father-in-law, and so Joseph is called the son of Heli, and the line thus completed. While Joseph was son-in-law of Heli, according to the flesh he was in actual fact the son of Jacob (Matthew 1:16).

6. Two genealogies are absolutely necessary to trace the lineage of our Lord and Saviour Jesus Christ, the one the royal and legal, the other the natural and literal; and these

two genealogies we find—the legal and royal in Matthew's
Gospel, the Gospel of law and kingship; the natural and literal in Luke's, the Gospel of humanity.

7. We are told in Jeremiah 22:30 that any descendant of
Jeconiah could not come to the throne of David. Joseph was
of this line, and while Joseph's genealogy furnishes the royal
line for Jesus, his son before the law, nevertheless Jeremiah's prediction is fulfilled to the very letter, for Jesus,
(strictly speaking) was not Joseph's descendant and therefore was not of the seed of Jeconiah. If Jesus had been the
son of Joseph in reality, He could not have come to the
throne, but He is Mary's son through Nathan and can come
to the throne legally by her marrying Joseph and so clearing
His way legally to it.

As we study these two genealogies of Jesus carefully and
read them in the light of Old Testament prediction, we find
that so far from constituting a reason for doubting the accuracy of the Bible they are rather a confirmation of the min-
utest accuracy of that Book. It is amazing how one part
of the Bible fits into another part when we study it thus
minutely. We need no longer stumble over the fact of two
genealogies, but discover and rejoice in the deep meaning of
the fact.

## XXI

## WAS JESUS REALLY THREE DAYS AND THREE NIGHTS IN THE HEART OF THE EARTH?

MATTHEW, in the twelfth chapter of his Gospel and the fortieth verse, reports Jesus as saying: "As Jonah was three days and three nights in the belly of the whale ("sea monster," R. V. margin), so shall the Son of man be three days and three nights in the heart of the earth." According to the commonly accepted tradition of the church Jesus was crucified on Friday, dying at 3 P. M., or somewhere between 3 P. M. and sundown, and was raised from the dead very early in the morning of the following Sunday. Many readers of the Bible are puzzled to know how the interval between late Friday afternoon and early Sunday morning can be figured out to be three days and three nights. It seems rather to be two nights, one day and a very small portion of another day.

The solution of this apparent difficulty proposed by many commentators is that "a day and a night" is simply another way of saying "a day," and that the ancient Jews reckoned a fraction of a day as a whole day, so they say there was a part of Friday (a very small part), or a day and a night; all of Saturday, another day, or a day and a night; part of Sunday (a very small part), another day, or a day and a night.

There are many persons whom this solution does not altogether satisfy, and the writer is free to confess it does not satisfy him at all. It seems to him to be a makeshift, and a very weak makeshift.

Is there any solution that is altogether satisfactory? There is.

The first fact to be noticed in the proper solution is that the Bible nowhere says or implies that Jesus was crucified

and died on Friday. It is said that Jesus was crucified on
"the day before the sabbath" (Mark 15:42). As the Jewish
weekly sabbath came on Saturday, beginning at sunset the
evening before, the conclusion is naturally drawn that as
Jesus was crucified the day before the sabbath He must have
been crucified on Friday. But it is a well-known fact, to
which the Bible bears abundant testimony, that the Jews had
other sabbaths beside the weekly sabbath which fell on Saturday. The first day of the Passover week, no matter upon
what day of the week it came, was always a sabbath
(Exodus 12:16; Leviticus 23:7; Numbers 28:16-18). The
question therefore arises whether the sabbath that followed
Christ's crucifixion was the weekly sabbath (Saturday) or
the Passover sabbath, falling on the 15th of Nisan, which
came that year on Thursday. Now the Bible does not leave
us to speculate in regard to which sabbath is meant in this
instance, for John tells us in so many words, in John 19:14,
that the day on which Jesus was tried and crucified was "the
preparation *of the Passover*" (R. V.), that is, it was not the
day before the weekly sabbath (Friday) but it was the day
before the Passover sabbath, which came that year on Thursday. That is to say, the day on which Jesus Christ was crucified was

### WEDNESDAY.

John makes this as clear as day.

The Gospel of John was written later than the other Gospels, and scholars have for a long time noticed that in various places there was an evident intention to correct false
impressions that one might get from reading the other Gospels. One of these false impressions was that Jesus ate the
Passover with His disciples at the regular time of the Passover. To correct this false impression John clearly states
that He ate it the evening before, and that He Himself died
on the cross *at the very moment* the Passover lambs were
being slain "between the two evenings" on the 14th Nisan

(Exodus 12:6, Hebrew and R. V. margin). God's real Pascal Lamb, Jesus, of whom all other pascal lambs offered through the centuries were only types, was therefore slain at the very time appointed of God.

Everything about the Passover lamb was

## FULFILLED IN JESUS.

(1) He was a Lamb without blemish and without spot (Exodus 12:5). (2) He was chosen on the 10th day of Nisan (Exodus 12:3), for it was on the tenth day of the month, the preceding Saturday, that the triumphal entry into Jerusalem was made, since they came from Jericho to Bethany six days before the Passover (John 12:1—that would be six days before Thursday, which would be Friday), and it was on the next day that the entry into Jerusalem was made (John 12:12 and following verses), that is, on Saturday, the 10th Nisan. It was also on this same day that Judas went to the chief priests and offered to betray Jesus for thirty pieces of silver (Matthew 26:6-16; Mark 14:3-11). As it was after the supper in the house of Simon the leper, and as the supper occurred late on Friday, that is, after sunset, or early on Saturday, after the supper would necessarily be on the 10th Nisan. This being the price set on Him by the chief priests, it was the buying or taking to them of a lamb which according to law must occur on the 10th Nisan. Furthermore, they put the exact value on the lamb that Old Testament prophecy predicted (Matthew 26:15, compare Zechariah 11:12). (3) Not a bone of Him was broken when He was killed (John 19:36, compare Exodus 12:46; Numbers 9:12; Psalm 34:20). (4) And He was killed on the 14th Nisan between the evenings, just before the beginning of the 15th Nisan at sundown (Exodus 12:6, R. V., margin).

If we take just exactly what the Bible says, viz., that Jesus was slain before the Passover sabbath, the type is marvellously fulfilled in every detail, but if we accept the traditional theory that Jesus was crucified on Friday, the type fails at many points.

Furthermore, if we accept the traditional view that Jesus was crucified on Friday and ate the Passover on the regular day of the Passover, then the journey from Jericho to Bethany, which occurred six days before the Passover (John 12:1) would fall on a Saturday, that is, the Jewish sabbath. Such a journey on the Jewish sabbath would be contrary to the Jewish law. Of course it was impossible for Jesus to take such a journey on the Jewish sabbath. In reality His triumphal entry into Jerusalem was on the Jewish sabbath, Saturday. This was altogether possible, for the Bible elsewhere tells us that Bethany was a sabbath day's journey from Jerusalem (Acts 1:12; compare Luke 24:50).

Furthermore, it has been figured out by the astronomers that in the year 30 A. D., which is the commonly accepted year of the crucifixion of our Lord, the Passover was kept on Thursday, April 6th, the moon being full that day. The chronologists who have supposed that the crucifixion took place on Friday have been greatly perplexed by this fact that in the year 30 A. D., the Passover occurred on Thursday. One writer in seeking a solution of the difficulty suggests that the crucifixion may have been in the year 33 A. D., for although the full moon was on a Thursday that year also, yet as it was within two and half hours of Friday, he thinks that perhaps the Jews may have kept it that day. But when we accept exactly what the Bible says, namely, that Jesus was not crucified on the Passover day but on "the preparation of the Passover," and that He was to be three days and three nights in the grave, and as "the preparation of the Passover" that year would be Wednesday and His resurrection early on the first day of the week, this allows exactly three days and three nights in the grave.

To sum it all up,

### JESUS DIED ABOUT SUNSET ON WEDNESDAY.

Seventy-two hours later, exactly three days and three nights, at the beginning of the first day of the week (Saturday at sunset), He arose again from the grave. When the women visited the tomb just before dawn next morning, they found the grave already empty. So we are not driven to any such makeshift as that any small portion of a day is reckoned as a whole day and night, but we find that the statement of Jesus was literally true. Three days and three nights His body was dead and lay in the sepulchre. While His body lay dead, He Himself being quickened in the spirit (1 Peter 3:18) went into the heart of the earth and preached unto the spirits which were in prison (1 Peter 3:19).

This supposed difficulty solves itself, as do so many other difficulties in the Bible, when we take the Bible as meaning exactly what it says.

It is sometimes objected against the view here advanced that the two on the way to Emmaus early on the first day of the week (that is, Sunday) said to Jesus in speaking of the crucifixion and events accompanying it: "Besides all this, today is the third day since these things were done" (Luke 24:21), and it is said that if the crucifixion took place on Wednesday, Sunday would be the fourth day since these things were done. But the answer is very simple. These things were done just as Thursday was beginning at sunset on Wednesday. They were therefore completed on Thursday, and the first day since Thursday would be Friday, the second day since Thursday would be Saturday, and "the third day since" Thursday would be Sunday, the first day of the week. So the supposed objection in reality supports the theory. On the other hand, if the crucifixion took place on Friday, by no manner of reckoning could Sunday be made "the third day since" these things were done.

There are

## MANY PASSAGES IN SCRIPTURE

that support the theory advanced above and make it necessary to believe that Jesus died late on Wednesday. Some of them are as follows: "For as Jonah was three days and three nights in the whale's belly, so shall the Son of Man be *three days and three nights* in the heart of the earth" (Matthew 12:40). "This fellow said, I am able to destroy the temple of God and to build it *in three days*" (Matthew 26:61). "Thou that destroyest the temple and buildest it in *three days*, save Thyself" (Matthew 27:40). "Sir, we remember that that deceiver said, while He was yet alive, *After three days* I will rise again" (Matthew 27:63). "The Son of Man must suffer many things, and be killed, and *after three days* rise again" (Mark 8:31). "They shall kill Him, and when He is killed, *after three days* He shall rise again" (Mark 9:31, R. V.). "They shall scourge Him, and shall kill Him, and *after three days* He shall rise again" (Mark 10:34, R. V.). "Destroy this temple that is made with hands, and *in three days* I will build another made without hands" (Mark 14:58, R. V.). "Ah, Thou that destroyest the temple and buildest it *in three days*, save Thyself!" (Mark 15:29). "Besides all this, today is *the third day since* these things were done" (Luke 24:21). "Jesus answered and said unto them, Destroy this temple, and *in three days* I will raise it up. Then said the Jews, Forty and six years was this temple in building, and wilt thou raise it up *in three days?* But He spake of the temple of His body. When therefore He was risen from the dead, His disciples remembered that He had said this, and they believed the Scripture and the word which Jesus had said" (John 2:19-22).

There is absolutely nothing in favor of Friday crucifixion, but everything in the Scripture is perfectly harmonized by Wednesday crucifixion. It is remarkable how many prophetical and typical passages of the Old Testament are fulfilled and how many seeming discrepancies in the Gospel narratives are straightened out when we once come to understand that Jesus died on Wednesday and not on Friday.

## XXII

## How Could Jesus Commend the Action of the Unrighteous Steward?

A very puzzling passage in the Bible to many is the story of the unrighteous steward recorded in Luke 16:1-14. Once when this passage was assigned by the International Sunday School Committee, a lady told me that she had made up her mind not to teach it. She said:

"The three points of difficulty are: First, that Jesus should hold this dishonest scoundrel up for our imitation; second, that the Lord should commend the unrighteous steward; and third, that Jesus should command the disciples to make themselves friends of the mammon of unrighteousness."

We will take up these three points in order. By noticing exactly what is said, we will soon see that in each point, if we adhere strictly to the very words of Jesus, the difficulty will disappear, and that the incident instead of staggering us will be found to be profoundly instructive along the line where instruction is greatly needed today.

1. Why did Jesus "hold this dishonest scoundrel up for our imitation"?

The answer is found in the text itself. Jesus did not hold him up for imitation.

He held him up, first of all, as a warning of what would overtake unfaithful stewards, how they would be called to give account of their stewardship, and their stewardship be taken from them.

Having taught this solemn and salutary lesson, one that is much needed today, Jesus went on to show how 'the sons of this world are *for their own generation* wiser than the sons of the light" (v. 8, R. V.). They are wiser at this point, for they use their utmost ingenuity and put forth their utmost effort to make present opportunities count for the hour of future need. "The sons of light" oftentimes do not do that. Indeed, how many twentieth century sons of light, who profess to believe that eternity is all and time is nothing in comparison, are using their utmost ingenuity and putting forth their utmost efforts to make the opportunity of the present life count most for the needs of the great eternity which is to follow?

## THE AVERAGE PROFESSED CHRISTIAN

today uses the utmost ingenuity and puts forth his utmost effort to bring things to pass in business and other affairs of this brief present world, but when it comes to matters that affect eternity he is content with the exercise of the least possible amount of ingenuity and with the putting forth of the smallest effort that will satisfy his conscience.

Jesus did not point to the steward's dishonesty to stir our emulation—He plainly rebuked his dishonesty, but He did point to his common sense in using the opportunity of the present to provide for the necessities of the future, and would have us learn to use the opportunities of the present to provide for the necessities of the future, the eternal future. Even in pointing out his common sense, Jesus carefully guarded His statement by saying that the unjust steward was "wiser *for his own generation*." He knew only the life that now is, and from that narrow and imperfect standpoint he was wiser than "the son of light" from his broad and true standpoint of knowing eternity, but an eternity for which he is not wise enough to live wholly.

There are other utterances of our Lord and Saviour, where wicked and selfish men are held up by way of contrast to show how much more godly men, or even God Himself, may be expected to act in the way suggested, for instance, Luke 18:6, 7; 11:5-8; Matthew 12:11, 12.

The first difficulty then in the passage has disappeared upon careful scrutiny of exactly what is said. Let us pass on to the second difficulty.

2. Why did the Lord "commend the unrighteous steward"?
The answer to this, too, is very simple, namely, that

### THE LORD JESUS DID NOT COMMEND

the unrighteous steward.

This is evident by a single glance at the Revised Version
of verse 8. In the Authorized Version, it is true, it reads:
"The lord commended the unrighteous steward." Now if
we were to leave it standing in that way there might be some
possible doubt as to whether "the lord" meant was the "lord"
mentioned in the passage, (the lord of the steward), or
whether it was the Lord Jesus, who relates the parable. The
Revised Version removes this possible ambiguity by trans-
lating "his lord" (that is, the steward's lord), who commended the unrighteous steward. It was not the Lord Jesus
who commended him, but his own lord, and he only commended his shrewdness. That the interpretation of the Revised Version is the correct interpretation of the verse is beyond dispute, for the Lord Jesus is the speaker, and it is
He that speaks about the one who does the commending as
"the lord," evidently not speaking about Himself, but about
the lord of the unjust steward. It is only by very careless
reading of the passage that anyone could make "the lord" of
this passage the Lord Jesus. The Lord Jesus, so far from
commending him, flatly calls him "the unrighteous steward,"
and furthermore just below warns against unfaithfulness in
stewardship (vs. 10, 11).

So the second difficulty entirely disappears on a careful
noticing of what is said. Let us pass on to the third difficulty.

3. Why does Jesus "command His disciples to make themselves friends of the mammon of unrighteousness"?
This difficulty disappears when we get

### THE CORRECT AND EXACT BIBLICAL DEFINITIONS

of the terms used.

First of all, what does "the mammon of unrighteousness" mean? It means nothing more or less than money. Money is called "the mammon of unrighteousness" because money is such a constant minister to sin and selfishness (as, for example, the case of the scoundrel above mentioned), and because "the love of money is a root of all kinds of evil" (1 Timothy 6:9, 10, R. V.). Jesus in passing would lift a word of warning against the perils of money by speaking of it as "the mammon of unrighteousness." He often packed a whole sermon into a single phrase.

In the second place, what does "of" mean when our Lord tells us to make to ourselves friends *"of"* the mammon of unrighteousness?

The answer to this question is found in the Revised Version, where "of" is properly rendered "by means of." So then what Jesus bade His disciples do (and what He bids us do) was to make themselves friends by means of money, that is to say, to so use the money God entrusted to them in the present life as to make friends for themselves by their use of it, and (as the context shows) to make these friends among God's poor and needy ones, who would go to the eternal "tabernacles" (v. 9, R. V.) and be ready to give us, their benefactors who had used our money to bless them, a royal welcome when our life here on earth is ended and so our money has failed. In other words, Jesus simply put into a new and striking form His oft-repeated teaching, not to keep our money hoarded, not to spend it on ourselves, but to spend it in doing good, especially to God's needy ones, and so invest it in heavenly and abiding securities (compare Matthew 6:19, 21; 19:21, 29; 25:40; 1 Timothy 6:17-19; Proverbs 19:17).

That this teaching of Jesus was clearly understood by His hearers is proved by v. 14 (R. V.) that follows. In this verse we are told that the Pharisees, "who were lovers of money, heard all these things, and they scoffed at Him" (R. V.).

So the third and last difficulty has disappeared, and this

passage stands out in glorious light, teaching with great force a lesson that our day greatly needs to learn, namely, that

## MONEY IS A STEWARDSHIP,

and that he who seeks to enjoy it in the brief present, and not rather so to expend it that it will bring him interest for all eternity, is a great fool, and even the petty shrewdness of "the sons of this world" rebukes him.

## XXIII

### WERE JESUS AND PAUL MISTAKEN AS TO THE TIME OF OUR LORD'S RETURN?

IT is constantly taught not only by unbelievers but even in many Christian pulpits and in some of our theological seminaries that Jesus and Paul were mistaken as to the time of our Lord's return. In an interesting little pamphlet published by the American Unitarian Association, in which five ministers, once preaching in orthodox churches but now Unitarians, tell how they became Unitarians, one writer says:

"But in a lecture one day on Thessalonians, our professor remarked that Paul evidently was mistaken as to the time of the coming of Christ. I was thunderstruck, and stared rigidly at the speaker, while my pencil dropped from my fingers. It is true, then, after all the denunciation of the preachers. Higher criticism isn't the false, shallow thing that it was made out to be. I can hear yet, after many years, the echo of that slamming book in the vacant library, and that cedar pencil clattering to the floor."

Evidently this young man was easily shaken. If a professor in a theological seminary said anything, that settled it for him. The professor must certainly be correct, and all other professors who taught differently, and all others who studied the Bible for themselves, must be wrong. The fact that the professor made such a remark as this was proof positive that higher criticism was not "the false, shallow thing it was made out to be." I do not wonder that such a young man should wind up as a Unitarian preacher. But even theological professors are sometimes mistaken, and this professor was mistaken. The mistake was altogether the professor's, and not at all Paul's, as we shall see in a few moments.

112

Let us begin with Jesus, and not with Paul.

## WAS JESUS MISTAKEN

as to the time of His own return? In proof that He was,
Matthew 24:34 and parallel passages in the other Gospels
(Mark 13:30; Luke 21:32) are constantly cited. Our Lord
is here reported as saying: "Verily, verily, I say unto you,
This generation shall not pass away until all these things be
accomplished" (Matthew 24:34, R. V.). And it is held that
Jesus here plainly teaches that the generation living on earth
at the time that He spoke these words would not have passed
away before all the things recorded in the preceding verses
had come to pass; and of course this would be a mistake.

But if anybody will read the entire passage carefully, he
will see that Jesus here teaches nothing of the kind. In the
context He is teaching

## HOW RAPIDLY THINGS WILL CULMINATE AT THE END,

that when certain signs begin to appear events will ripen so
fast that the generation then living when these signs appear,
will not have passed away until all things belonging to that
particular epoch shall have come to be. These signs mentioned as indicating the speedy close of the age are found in
verse 29,—the sun darkened, the moon not giving her light,
stars falling from heaven, and the powers of heaven shaken.
These signs did not occur while our Lord was on earth, nor
in that generation, but when they do occur, then things will
ripen so fast that the sign of the Son of man shall be seen
in heaven, and the Son of man shall come in clouds with
power and great glory before the generation then existing
passes away.

That this is the true interpretation of the passage is evident from verse 33, where Jesus says distinctly: *"When ye
see all these things* know ye that He is nigh, even at the
doors"* (R. V. and v. 32). Here Jesus teaches that just as

8

the putting forth of tender shoots and young leaves is an indication that summer is nigh, so the appearing of these signs will be an indication that the Lord is nigh, so nigh that that generation will not pass away until the Lord actually comes. And "this generation" of verse 34 clearly refers, if taken in the context, to the generation existing when these signs shall appear.

The connection is just the same in Mark 13, where similar words are found. If possible, it is even clearer in Luke 21:25-32, where the words are found again. So the whole difficulty is not with what Jesus actually said, but with the failure of expositors to carefully notice exactly what the thought in mind was when Jesus uttered the words to which objection has been made.

### ANOTHER INTERPRETATION OF THIS VERSE

has been offered which is full of suggestion, namely, that the word rendered "generation" in this passage means oftentimes "race" or "family," "men begotten of the same stock," and this doubtless is the meaning of the word used. In fact this is the meaning given as the second meaning of the word in Thayer's *Greek-English Lexicon of the New Testament*, and the meaning of "age" (or "generation") is the fourth meaning given. Taking this as the meaning of the word, the passage is interpreted to mean that this "race" or generation (that is, the Jewish race) shall not pass away (that is, shall maintain its race identity) until the coming of the Lord. It is a remarkable fact,—indeed, one of the most remarkable facts of history,—that though the Jews have for centuries been driven from their native land and scattered throughout all the nations, they have always retained their race identity. This thought may also have been in Jesus' mind, and the utterance thus have been a pregnant utterance with a fulness of meaning that cannot be exhausted by one interpretation. But from the context, the primary meaning seems to be the one given in the first explanation above.

Another passage urged to show that Jesus was mistaken about the time of His return is Matthew 16:28: "Verily, I say unto you, there be some standing here that shall not taste of death till they see the Son of man coming in His kingdom." (See also the parallel passages, Mark 9:1; Luke 9:27.) It is held that in this passage Jesus teaches that His coming again would be before some of those standing there should die.

But here again in the context is found the entire solution of the difficulty. There ought to be no chapter division where Matthew 17 begins (the chapter divisions are not a part of the original Scriptures, and there should be no chapter division here). We should read right on as we do in the parallel passages in Mark and Luke, and if we read right on and notice what is said, the meaning of Jesus' words becomes as clear as day. The words were spoken as

## A Prophecy of the Transfiguration,

the account of which immediately follows with the closely connecting article "And." Three of those standing with Jesus when He spoke the words were to go up with Him into the mount, and there in the mount they were to see His true glory shining forth in His face, in His person, in the very raiment He wore (Matthew 17:2), they were to hear the Father declare: "This is My beloved Son, in whom I am well pleased" (v. 6). In all this they saw "the Son of man coming in His kingdom." If events had been allowed to take their natural course, Jesus then and there would have been manifested to the world as He was to the disciples, as King; but Jesus chose rather, in order that men might be saved, to go down from this mount of transfiguration where He was manifested in His glory as coming in His kingdom, where the kingdom of God came with power (Mark 9:1), where Peter and James and John saw the kingdom of God (Luke 9:27), to die as an atoning sacrifice on the cross of Cavalry. It is a significant fact in this connection that the subject of which Moses and Elijah, who appeared talking with Him in the mount, spoke was the decease which He should accomplish at Jerusalem (Luke 9:31).

Here again then we see that the mistake was not on Jesus' part, but arises from the carelessness of the interpreter in overlooking the context in which the words of Jesus are found, and the interpretation that is put upon the words by the writers themselves immediately after they have recorded them. So all these arguments of the destructive critics built upon our Lord's being mistaken as to the time of His own return, fall to the ground.

### But was not Paul Mistaken?

It is constantly said that he was by those who contend against the verbal accuracy of the New Testament writings. It is said over and over again that "Paul evidently was mistaken in his early writings as to the time of the coming of Christ." In defense of this contention the words of Paul contained in 1 Thessalonians 4:15-18, R. V., are brought forward. Paul here says: "For this we say unto you by the word of the Lord that we which are alive and remain unto the coming of the Lord shall in no wise precede them that are fallen asleep," etc. It is said that these words make it evident that Paul expected to be alive when the Lord came.

What Paul may have expected I do not know. Very likely he did hope to be alive when the Lord came, but he certainly did not teach that he would be alive, and no one holds any theory of inspiration that maintains that the Bible writers did not entertain mistaken hopes. All that the one who contends for the plenary theory of inspiration and absolute veracity and accuracy of Bible teaching is that the Bible writers nowhere teach error. That they may have entertained erroneous notions on a great many things no one questions. All that is maintained is that if they had such erroneous notions, the Holy Spirit kept them from teaching them.

Paul certainly does not teach here that he would be alive

when the Lord came. He does teach that some persons would have fallen asleep and others would be alive. As he was still alive, he naturally put himself in the class to which he belonged at the time of writing, "Those which are alive" (that are left). He certainly was alive at the time. He certainly was one of those left at that time. That he should continue to be alive he does not say. Very likely he hoped to be. Every believer who has a true understanding of the doctrine of the coming of the Lord naturally entertains a hope that he may be alive when the Lord comes. I hope that I may be, but not for a moment do I venture to teach that I will be, but I do know that I am alive at this moment. I know that I am not one of those who have as yet fallen asleep, and if I were differentiating between the two classes, those who are alive and those who are fallen asleep, I should certainly put myself with those who are alive, and would not be mistaken in so doing. Paul knew perfectly well that the Lord Himself had taught long before he wrote these words to the Thessalonians that it is not for us to know times or seasons which the Father hath set within His own authority (Acts 1:7, R. V.). He did not attempt to know times or seasons which his Master had so distinctly taught it was not for him, or for us, to know; but he did teach by "the word of the Lord" Himself that "the Lord Himself shall descend from heaven with a shout, with the voice of the archangel and the trump of God, and the dead in Christ shall rise first. Then we which are alive and remain shall be caught up together with them in the clouds to meet the Lord in the air, and so shall we ever be with the Lord." In the context, verses 13 and 14, Paul is urging those who are alive (and are left) at that time not to sorrow over those who had already fallen asleep, and as he was among the class that were alive (that were left) up to that time, he naturally and properly and correctly put himself with them and not with those over whom they were not to sorrow, namely, those who had already fallen asleep.

So in this passage instead of finding that the Holy Spirit left Paul to make mistakes, in point of fact the Holy Spirit

### KEPT HIM FROM MAKING A MISTAKE

even in regard to the matter about which in his own longing he might have entertained a mistaken hope. The whole passage then instead of being an argument against the verbal accuracy of the Scriptures is an argument for it, and shows how the men whom the Holy Spirit chose to be the vehicles of His revelation to us were kept absolutely from putting into their teaching any mistaken hope which they might have entertained. Our critical friends who are hunting so persistently for some mistake in the teaching of Paul will have to carry their search farther, and possibly the experience of the young theological student that was so thunderstruck by his professor in the orthodox school saying that Paul was mistaken as to the time of the coming of Christ and who therefore launched forth into Unitarianism, may learn to be cautious lest his teaching prove equally disastrous to some other weak-minded young men.

## XXIV

**DID JESUS GO INTO THE ABODE OF THE DEAD, AND PREACH TO THE SPIRITS IN PRISON? AND IS THERE ANOTHER PROBATION AFTER DEATH?**

I THINK I have never had a question box in any city but someone put in the question: "What does I Peter 3:18-20 mean when it says that Jesus went and preached unto the spirits in prison?"

A very simple answer to this question is that it means just exactly what it says. But let us notice carefully exactly what it does say:

"Because Christ also suffered for sins once, the righteous for the unrighteous, that He might bring us to God; being put to death in the flesh, but quickened in the spirit; in which also He went and preached unto the spirits in prison, which aforetime were disobedient, when the longsuffering of God waited in the days of Noah, while the ark was a-preparing, wherein few, that is, eight souls, were saved through water" (R. V.).

The point of difficulty with this passage with many people is the thought that seems to be conveyed that Jesus actually went into the abode of the dead and there preached to spirits in prison; and this would seem to imply to many that there is an opportunity for repentance after death.

Many have attempted to explain the verses, in order to avoid this conclusion, by saying that the spirit here mentioned in which Jesus was quickened is the Holy Spirit, and that in the Holy Spirit Jesus Christ preached through Noah while the ark was preparing to the spirits which were then disobedient and who consequently are now in prison.

One writer, William Kelly, has argued for this interpretation with a great deal of ability and skill and with a large display of knowledge of Greek grammar. Of Mr. Kelly's

119

unusual knowledge of Greek there can be no question, but none the less I think he fails to make out his case. After all has been said, it seems to me this interpretation is an evasion.

"The spirit" in verse 18 cannot mean the Holy Spirit.

A contrast is being drawn between the two parts of Christ's nature, the flesh in which He was put to death and the spirit in which He was quickened (that is, made alive) at the time He was put to death in the flesh. In His spirit in which He was made alive, while the body lay motionless in death, He went and preached unto the spirits in prison. It seems to me that this is

### The Only Fair Interpretation

to put upon the words, and if we are to take the Scriptures as meaning exactly what they say, this is what we must take them as meaning.

But does not this involve

### A Second Probation

for those who have died in disobedience to God and who consequently have gone to the place of penalty and suffering? Even if it did, we ought not to dodge it on that account, we ought to be fair with the Scriptures whether they conform to our theories or not. But in point of fact, this does not in any wise involve a second probation for those who have died in disobedience and who consequently have gone to the place of penalty and suffering.

This is apparent if we notice three things: First, if we notice to whom Jesus preached; second, if we notice what He preached to them; and third, if we notice what were the results of His preaching.

First of all, then,

### To Whom Did Jesus Preach?

"The spirits in prison." But who were these spirits in prison?

Were they the spirits of departed wicked men? There is nothing whatever to indicate that they were. The word "spirits" is never used in this unqualified way of the spirits of departed men, but it is used constantly of angelic or super-natural beings (Hebrews 1:7, 14; Matthew 10:1; Mark 3:11; Luke 6:18; 7:21; Acts 19:12; 1 John 4:1; and many other places). The only place in Scripture where "spirits" is used of men in any way analogous to this is Hebrews 12:23. The constant use is of angels or other supernatural beings. If we so interpret it here, the preaching was not at all to men who had been wicked in the days of Noah but to supernatural beings who had been disobedient in the days of Noah and who were now in prison in consequence of this disobedience. Are there any Scripture passages that hint that there were supernatural beings who were disobedient in the days of Noah and who were consequently now in prison? There are. In Genesis 6:1 we are told that "the sons of God saw the daughters of men that they were fair, and they took them wives of all which they chose." By "the sons of God" in this passage many commentators understand the descendants of Seth, a godly man, but if we are to interpret Scripture by Scripture they seem rather to have been angelic beings. There seems to be a clear reference to this passage in Jude 6, where we are told of "angels which kept not their own principality but left their proper habitation" and in consequence were kept in everlasting chains in darkness into the judgment of the great day (R. V.), and in the next verse we are told that Sodom and Gomorrah *in like manner* with these (that is, these angels) gave themselves over to fornication and went after strange flesh (R. V.). Now from this it seems clear that the sin of the angels was going after strange flesh, the very sin mentioned in Genesis 6:2. Furthermore, we read in 2 Peter that "God spared not the angels that sinned but cast them down to hell and committed them to darkness to be reserved unto judgment" (2 Peter 2:3, 4, R. V.). The clear implication of all this is that the spirits to whom Jesus preached when He went to the abode of the dead were the angels that sinned in the days of Noah and who were then in prison in consequence of that sin.

Let us notice, in the next place,

## What the Word Translated "Preach"

in 1 Peter 3:18-20 means. There are two words in constant use in the New Testament which are translated "preach." One means "to preach the Gospel," the other "to herald," to herald the king or kingdom. It is the latter of these two words which is used in this passage. There is not a suggestion in the passage that the Gospel with its offer of salvation was preached to anyone. The King and the kingdom were heralded. So then even if we take "the spirits in prison" to mean the spirits of men who had died in sin, there is not a hint of another probation. We are simply told that the King and the kingdom were heralded to them. Christ has been heralded as King in heaven, earth and hell.

In the third place, notice

## The Results of this Preaching.

There is not a word of suggestion that any of the spirits in prison were converted by it. If they were we must learn it from other sources than this passage, but there is not a single passage anywhere in the Scriptures that suggests that there were any conversions or any salvation resultant from this preaching. The purpose of the preaching evidently was not the salvation of those already lost but the proclamation of the kingdom and the King throughout the universe. The time is coming when every knee shall bow, of things in heaven and things on earth and things under the earth, and every tongue shall confess that Jesus Christ is Lord, to the glory of God the Father (Philippians 2:10, 11). But that enforced confession of Christ on the part of disobedient men and angels will bring them no salvation. We must all take our choice of either confessing and accepting Christ of our own free will now and obtaining salvation thereby, or of confessing Him and acknowledging Him against our will in the world to come. Confess Him we must sometime. Bow the knee to Him we must some day. Happy the man who gladly now in this time of probation bows the knee to Jesus and confesses that Jesus Christ is Lord to the glory of God the Father, and does not wait until that day when he is forced to do it and when the confession will bring him no salvation!

# INDEX OF BIBLE TEXTS

122

# The Moody COLPORTAGE Library

Uniform in size and style, attractive paper covers, 4¾ x 6¾ inches. 20c each.

**Ask for descriptive folder.**

THE MOODY PRESS
153 Institute Place (Dept. MCL)
Chicago

# The Evangel Booklets

BRIEF, TIMELY messages of supreme importance, and gospel stories, by evangelical preachers and teachers, Christian workers and laymen. Prayerful co-operation of distribution solicited. 32-page booklets, self-cover.

1. **God Is Love.** An appeal to the unsaved. **D. L. Moody.**
2. **God Reaching Down.** Messages to the unconverted. **C. H. Spurgeon.**
4. **Jack Winsted's Choice.** A Gospel story. **Lillian E. Andrews.**
6. **Ruined, Redeemed, Regenerated.** **C. H. Mackintosh.**
7. **By the Old Mill.** Story. **Katherine Elise Chapman.**
8. **The Day After Thanksgiving.** Story. **Mrs. S. R. Graham Clark.**
9. **True Stories About God's Free Gift.** **Alexander Marshall.**
10. **Lois Dudley Finds Peace.** Story. **Anna Potter Wright.**
12. **The Penitent Thief, and Naaman the Syrian.** **D. L. Moody.**
13. **Adder's Eggs and Spider's Webs.** **H. A. Ironside.**
14. **Samuel Morris.** The true story of a Spirit-filled African.
16. **Saved and Safe.** Salvation, Assurance and Security. **Fred J. Meldau.**
17. **"In the Beginning God—" and other Talks.** **Mark A. Matthews.**
18. **Christian Science: Pedigree, Principles, Posterity. Percy W. Stephens.**
19. **Modern Education at the Cross-Roads.** **M. H. Duncan.**
20. **Is the Bible True?** Nashville address. **Wm. Jennings Bryan.**
21. **The Public Reading of the Word of God.** **A. T. Pierson.**
22. **"The Most Important Thing in My Life."** The testimony of Dr. Howard A. Kelly, world-famous surgeon. **William S. Dutton.**
23. **Where Are the Dead?** **H. C. Marshall.**
24. **Gold from Ophir.** Homilies. **Northcote Deck.**
25. **Mary Antipas.** Story. **Howard W. Pope.**
26. **Four Old Pals.** Story. **Frederick Burnham.**
28. **Dios es Amor (God Is Love).** Spanish edition of No. 1.
29. **Forethought in Creation.** **W. Bell Dawson.**
30. **Bryan's Last Word on Evolution.** **William Jennings Bryan.**
31. **Why I Do Not Believe in the Organic Evolutionary Hypothesis.** **James Edward Congdon.**
33. **The Double Cure.** A Gospel appeal. **Melvin E. Trotter.**
35. **Old Truths for Young Lives.** For children.
37. **How to Have a Happy Home.** **Harold Francis Branch.**
38. **The Peril of Unbelief and the Danger of Doubt.** **D. L. Moody.**
39. **Moody the Evangelist.** **Joseph B. Bowles.**
40. **The Only Begotten Son.** **H. A. Ironside.**
42. **Tom Bennett's Transformation.** Story. **Howard W. Pope.**
43. **Will a God of Love Punish Any of His Creatures Forever?** **Alexander Marshall.**
45. **Intercession for Revival.** **Helen C. Alexander Dixon.**
46. **With Everlasting Love.** Story. **Elzoe Prindle Stead.**
47. **How the Word Works.** **Fred J. Meldau.**
48. **Why I Believe the Bible.** **M. H. Duncan.**
49. **Caught.** Story. **C. S. Knight.**
50. **The Fruit of the Spirit Is Joy.** **John R. Riebe.**
51. **A Life Decision in the Sand Hills.** Story. **Ronald R. Kratz.**
52. **Love's Danger Signal.** **John G. Reid.**
53. **Pictures That Talk, Series One.** **E. J. Pace.**
54. **Pictures That Talk, Series Two.** **E. J. Pace.**
56. **My One Question Answered: Was Jesus Christ a Great Teacher Only?** **R. D. Sheldon.**
57. **Modern Miracles of Grace.** **John Wilmot Mahood.**
58. **How to Study the Bible.** A helpful outline. **B. B. Sutcliffe.**
59. **What is Your Answer?** **Oswald J. Smith.**
60. **Deus E Amor (God Is Love)** Portuguese edition of No. 1.
61. **The True and False in Christian Work and Worship.** **M. H. Duncan.**
62. **What Must I Do to be Saved?** **George E. Guille.**
63. **The Man in the Well.** Other religious faiths. **Oswald J. Smith.**
64. **Why All "Good People" Will Be Lost.** **J. E. Conant.**
65. **Two in One.** Believer's two natures. **Herbert Lockyer.**
66. **The Compromise Road.** Story. **Paul Hutchens.**
67. **An Hundredfold.** Stewartship. **David McConoughy.**
68. **Death or Life, Which?** A clear presentation. **Oswald J. Smith.**
69. **Bernard Enters the Race.** Story. **Anna Potter Wright.**
70. **The Trial of Jesus.** **Harold F. Branch.**
71. **The Christian's Citizenship.** **M. H. Duncan.**
72. **Atheism and the Bible.** A startling revelation. **Oswald J. Smith.**
73. **Galatians.** God's answer to legalism. **B. B. Sutcliffe.**
74. **O Sangue.** (The Blood) Portuguese. **D. L. Moody.**
75. **Who is a Christian?** Timely questions answered. **Oswald J. Smith.**
76. **Broken Life-Line.** Story. **Paul Hutchens.**

**Each, 10c; 12 copies (any assortment), $1.00; 100, $7.00.**

Attractive rates on large quantities.

## THE MOODY PRESS

153 Institute Place  Chicago, Ill., U.S.A.

# BIBLE LESSONS IN BIBLE ORDER

### (For Teachers of Children)

### By Mrs. Frank Hamilton

Vol.   I: The Pentateuch
Vol.  II: Joshua to Solomon
Vol. III: The Kingdoms of Israel and Judah:
      *Concluding lessons from the Old Testament*
Vol. IV: The Life of Christ—
      *Matthew, Mark, Luke, John*
Vol.  V: The Acts of the Apostles *and Program Material*

WITH the use of the blackboard and objects, the lessons in Bible order, beginning with Genesis, are taught in a way that the child can *see* them as well as *hear* them, and thus be able to *retain* them.

Each lesson begins with a Golden Text, which may be used as a memory verse, after which the story is told in a manner that will interest the young. At the close of each section, blackboard suggestions are given. There are maps and pages of blackboard drawings.

Teachers of the Beginners, Primary and Junior grades in Sunday Schools and Vacation Bible Schools, as well as parents in the home, who recognize the importance of following a *consecutive* course of Bible lessons, will find these books of great value. They are practical and true to the Word. They are full of suggestions that can be developed by the skilful teacher.

Mrs. Hamilton is an exceptionally successful teacher of children. She had charge of Primary and Junior Departments of large and successful Sunday Schools for many years. She has been Superintendent of Instruction of a Primary Sunday School Teachers' Union. Summer Bible Schools have also come within the author's experience.

Vols. I, II, III and V, 112 pages each; Vol. IV, 144 pages
Durable Art Stock Covers. Each, 50 Cents

### THE MOODY PRESS

153 Institute Place           Chicago, Ill., U.S.A.